How to Save the World and Still be Home for Dinner

How to Save the World and Still be Home for Dinner

✦

A Day in the Life of an Awakening Mind

D'Angelo

iUniverse, Inc.
New York   Bloomington

How to Save the World and Still be Home for Dinner
A Day in the Life of an Awakening Mind

iUniverse books may be ordered through booksellers or by contacting:

iUniverse
1663 Liberty Drive
Bloomington, IN 47403
www.iuniverse.com
1-800-Authors (1-800-288-4677)

Because of the dynamic nature of the Internet, any Web addresses or links contained in this book may have changed since publication and may no longer be valid.

ISBN: 978-1-4502-6879-0 (sc)
ISBN: 978-1-4502-6880-6 (ebk)

Printed in the United States of America

iUniverse rev. date: 11/8/2010

To Robert who created the space to allow change to happen, to the best parents and siblings one could be blessed with and to my children and their children and all the children of the world. Thank you for being my greatest teachers.

Contents

Preface

A few years ago I was having a conversation with my six-year-old grandson. "Francesco, what would you do to save the world?" I asked. He thought for a moment; "Grandma, I would have everyone be nice to each other."

Francesco's answer was clear and simple, but I soon discovered that to *be nice* was far more complex than I supposed.

I looked up the word in several dictionaries and found that in Middle English it meant *strange, lazy, foolish.* That wasn't quite what I was expecting, so I researched the original meaning of *nice*, and found that it comes from the Latin *nescire*; *ne* (*not*) + *scire* (*know*) = *to not know; to be ignorant.*

The contemporary English also proved to be interesting. The definitions were varied and a little more recognizable, but they started with the word *delicate,* followed by *precise, subtle, calling for great care, able to make delicate distinctions, scrupulous,* etc. Various other terms followed that: *agreeable; pleasant, virtuous, courteous, in good taste,* etc.

But it was the Latin root of *nice* that intrigued me *not to know.* I began to explore how it fit in with the concept of healing our world. Most of us are not too keen on performing great acts of heroism or spending our hard earned money to "save the world," nor do we have the time or energy necessary to really put ourselves out there, *but* it has been ingrained in us since childhood that we are toward "be nice."

After a lot of contemplation and with the urging of my inner voice, I share these thoughts with you. Hopefully this little book will speak to you directly. Perhaps it will awaken in you what you already know and offer you greater understanding of your path. It may even help you discover why you are here on this planet, and more, why you are here at this moment.

I've written for everyone who has asked, "What can I do to help change the world around me?" This book is for those—and I am one—who are no longer comfortable being an observer to man's inhumanity towards man. It is for us who wish to become more responsible stewards of our planet. For those who ache when we see children being mistreated and abandoned by society. It is for us who feel impotent as we witness the fear and violence in our world. It is for all of us who long to live in a world that is a safe and peaceful place for ourselves, for our children, and our children's children. It is for those of us who have felt compassion for another and have thought in silence or have spoken the words, "How can I help?"

We are all aware that there is no longer any place to hide from the world's issues. The world's problems are now our problems, right in our backyards, in our homes through the immediacy of our electronic media, in our schools, in our workplace, on our streets, in our environment, in our hearts, and also in our pocketbooks.

We've a longing deep inside to do *some*thing, but we are not quite sure what it is that we're supposed to be doing. Our circumstances get in the way—family commitments, job responsibilities, personal health, lack of financial resources, we're too tired, have no energy, "my plate is too full," and most of us cannot face being forced to fit one more thing into our already tightly compressed day.

Yet we feel that there should be *more*, something *different*. For some of us there is a longing, a deep emptiness that cries to be filled. We are simply numbed out, emotions frozen, passion for life depleted. We are just trying to get by day by day. We are putting in time, and we're not quite sure for what. We struggle to find our path in life, to understand our soul's journey. We wonder if this really is all there is. We question our circumstances and ask why.

It is said that there are no mistakes in the universe, that we are exactly where we are supposed to be. If we set our intent on finding our path, even though we feel *stuck* in our personal circumstances, we may discover ourselves seeing with new eyes, finding for the first time the incredible choices open to us—choices that will assist us in creating the change we long for. We may also discover that the problem lies in having the courage and the wisdom to choose.

There are those among us who have been touched by a glimmer of light that speaks of an awakening, an epiphany, a moment of deep joy where we just "know what we know." Our perspective shifts with the knowledge that things *could* be different, that there *could* be peace. Many of us have sat with that feeling for a very long time. But we have also sat with our impotence, confused in the chaos, feeling that we have lost the freedom to choose. We long for answers, for some direction, for simplicity, for some quiet, some peace. We want something more, but we are not quite sure what that *more* is. We feel an urgency, a need to do something, but we aren't sure what it is we need to do, where to start, where to go, or whom to ask.

This book does not attempt to teach, and it does not tell you anything new. Nor does it claim to resolve all or any of these feelings of longing and inadequacy. Everything here has been said and written over and over again in many forms by great masters and far more enlightened beings than I. Others have told us before that the answers are there, that they have always been there waiting patiently for us to remember them. Unfortunately, we seem unable to lift the blinders and recognize what we are looking for. We are not even clear as to what the real questions are.

This book is not about being "chosen" or "more enlightened." It is my belief that everyone has all knowledge, all knowingness, that the word *special* loses all meaning, because we are all from the same source. The answer to the question of why some are more enlightened may lie in the question of desire: "Just how conscious or awakened do I choose to be?"

"Awakened." "Conscious." These words are key to what I wish to say. And they lead to the word "mindful." As we become more *mindful*, we learn to share our minds, our thoughts, our actions with others, and others in turn pass them on. We pass them on in our own way—through the spoken or written word, through actions, feelings, or simply through being as centered and mindful. However one does it, the ripple effect that occurs affects everyone and everything around us.

Somewhere deep inside each of us is our truth—is *all* truth. I am nudging us toward remembering all that we are and all that we know, hoping to assist in removing the obstacle that keeps us in our deep sleep, perhaps to rid us of at least a bit of our tunnel vision, to help us take off our blinders and awaken to who we truly are and why we are here. This does not mean that we have to change anything, that we need to give away our money or our possessions. (If you feel moved to do something of that kind, then I would ask you to reconsider the intent and purpose behind your choice.) We don't need to join anything. We don't need to leave our families, quit our jobs, lose ourselves in a monastery, follow a guru or religious leader. We only need to change our perceptions, to change how we see and feel about ourselves.

I am addressing this in a rather simplistic way, when in reality, it can be as difficult, as painful, and as time-consuming as we wish to make it. We hang on to past ways by our fingertips and cling to all our old fears and pain and dis-ease because it is what we think we know. Our ego or false self screams loud and clear and makes every attempt to reinforce the things we've always believed, which, in essence is *who we are not*.

"Why bother in the first place?" we ask. "Given my circumstances, I can't make a difference anyway. Nobody is going to listen to me, or hear me, or care what I have to say. Who am I to think I can make a change?"

If that's the way you see it, you are absolutely right. And yes, it will involve giving up something; it will actually involve giving up a lot. You may need to give up how you think, see, and feel about yourself.

We cling fondly to old perceptions of who we are, perceptions based on the views of others—our parents, siblings, teachers, etc. We could call the change those external influences brought about in us, "our domestication." Our persona—the mask we wear before the world, and even when we are alone—is usually the result of things that have happened to us, or what we *perceived* happened to us. We take pride in "knowing ourselves" through what we do and what we think we see. But others have contributed greatly to our thoughts about our personal world and about ourselves.

When we put these influences aside and have another peek at our *real* self, we come to understand what a perception change really means, and the results are astounding. Everything changes simply because our perception has shifted.

The French philosopher Proust once said to his students, "I cannot change your circumstances, but I can help you see with new eyes." As you begin to see with new eyes, you reclaim your life and you "gain the whole world."

In fact, according to the teachings of Carl Yung, you reclaim your Self. This I can promise.

This little book is written as a simple guideline. I hope that in its simplicity, it will assist you in being part of this wonderful change of consciousness that is happening all around us. There have been those in every century who said they were living in interesting times. But I believe that we—you and I—are truly living in the most interesting time of all. We now have the technology, the power, and the ability to self-destruct or to bring peace and prosperity to the world, and what could be more interesting than that?

Socrates is alleged to have said that "the unexamined life is not worth living." To make our lives worth living, let's start this journey together by examining our lives with new eyes, by becoming more mindful, more awake, thereby reinforcing the truth that the world is indeed a much better place because you and I showed up.

It is time to truly *know ourselves*!

Chapter 1
Whose World Is This Anyway?

We ask ourselves: Who am I to be brilliant, gorgeous, talented, fabulous? Who are you not to be? Your playing small does not serve the world. There is nothing enlightened about shrinking so that others won't feel insecure around you. We were born to make manifest the glory of God that is within us. It's not just in some of us: it's in everyone.

—Nelson Mandela

"Playing small does not serve the world."

My world is different from yours simply because I am not in your mind, and I do not have the same perceptions as you. To explain my world to you would be to share knowledge, to share words that you would interpret from your own life's experience. So I cannot share the essence of my world, just as I cannot enter your mind to discover and completely understand your world. It would be like my trying to tell you what a green apple tastes like. The taste buds are mine, and the perceptions of tartness or sweetness, and the very words would be mine as well.

You *nescire* (do not know) about me except through your own perceptions, and I *nescire* (do not know) about you except through my perception of you. But we find ourselves in this cosmic soup together. How can it be just "my world" when we find ourselves sharing this life, this planet, and how can I/we *be nice* to ourselves and to each other to create change?

Humans like to think that they are guided by solid facts, but Andy Newberg, a University of Pennsylvania neuroscientist and professor of religious studies points out that all those so-called facts are actually beliefs. The 100 billion neurons in our brains take in an unending stream of information—say, the lines, shapes and contours activating cells in our eyes—and create a vivid 3-D image of a room with chairs and tables that allow us to navigate without crashing into things.

We are *born* to believe, Newberg says; consequently, we really don't have a choice. In his groundbreaking book *Why We Believe What We Believe,*

1

published by Simon & Shuster, Newberg details his conviction that studying belief is "the single most important quest" in neuroscience. His Holy Grail is to discover the grounds of *religious* belief, given its profound influence over history and the fact that our brains "privilege" it, by which he means, our brains give religious concerns ultimate priority.

"Spiritual realities, spiritual visions," he explains, "are reported by those who experience them as more real than real—not at all like a dream, which we recognize as an inferior reality when we wake. All we have to go on is what feels real to people: perception in the brain is all there is, and that forces us scientists to take it seriously."[1]

His tool is brain scans. Scientists cannot—yet—see belief, but imagining techniques can trace its path, the lit-up neural *experience* of belief. Newberg himself is genuinely on the fence. He is always conscious that perception is the only reality we can know, at least for now. "I think in the end there may be a way to 'prove' reality," he says. "But it will require us to follow both paths, the scientific and the spiritual."

The world that I perceive as my world, or the world that you perceive through your brain neurons, may differ from mine—our beliefs may be different. That does not mean that my world is better than yours, only that we have different perceptions based upon our different circumstances and how we "privilege" those perceptions. The truth may be that the only person I really can be *nic*e to is myself, in my world, and the same may go for you in your world—you being nice to you, but once we are nice to ourselves, we can't be unkind to each other, despite our perceptual differences. Check the definitions again and choose those that speak to you and start applying them to yourself to see what happens. I rather like the word "delicate." Today I will be "delicate" with myself.

Let's ask ourselves these questions. "How is my world today? How *nice* or delicate am I being with me? Is there anything I would like to change about my world as I know it? What role would I like to play?—a role of my own making. And how will my world be a better place because I showed up and started being nice to me?

I think most everyone has an inkling that he or she is not alone on this planet, even though there are times when we *feel* alone. Some of us have experienced that "journey into the darkness of the soul" in which we felt abandoned and separate from others. We may spend a lifetime looking for someone, something outside of ourselves to feed that emptiness. We get caught in the "if only" cure. If only we can find a soul mate; if my parents would only … ; if my partner or spouse would only …; if my children would only …; if my boss or my job would only …; if only I would win the lottery—the constant, never-ending search to fill that gnawing hunger never seems to abate.

Our Very Own Movie

We set up the illusion—as illusory as a movie that we are watching in a theater—and the movie's tragic theme is lack. And that *sense* of lack becomes our reality. It becomes our core belief, and we continue to recreate this in our life as our movie plays itself out.

But why? How did we get into this theater anyway? And why do we make it so difficult to leave? Let's take a look at this movie we find our selves collectively trapped into watching.

We see ourselves arriving naked in a space suit that we call our body, and from the first, we find that it doesn't function very well. It comes without instructions, no user manual. There is no one who rushes forward to give us hints.

Some of us are given a set of parents, some are not. Some stay with us, some leave. Some of us have siblings, some of us do not. The circumstances in which we find ourselves are varied and individuated. Some are set down in places that are not safe; some of these places are downright scary and dangerous while others are warm and nurturing.

We may ask, "How come he has loving parents and I don't?" "How does it happen she has everything that I want?"

So the questions go on. How did I end up with someone who sees me as a burden? How is it that we are constantly struggling to keep it together, but can barely survive? How did it come about that I get beaten and abused, and you are loved and spoiled? My legs or your arms don't work properly; my space suit is short, fat, tall, too skinny, and look—yours seems perfect. What's wrong with my space suit anyway? Why did I end up here? What am I supposed to be? *Who* am I supposed to be? Where am I expected to go? If anyone is listening, I am hiding in plain sight, so please come and help me!

And so, watching our arrival on film, we feel alone.

But let's do two things. Let us assume that we are *not* alone, that there is help, that there has always been help. Having been given this thing called "free will" and "choice," we are in a bit of a conundrum. The help that is present and waiting is able to do nothing for us unless we ask. That just seems to be the way it is.

So let's ask. But how and what do we ask for?

Before we get on with our journey, I have a question to ask you. "What's your deal with God—or Higher Power or Great Creator?" Or whatever name applies to this *something more*, this something that is all permeating, the something that gives us a sense of purpose, a feeling that we are here for more than to just be born, work hard, play a bit, and then die. Perhaps our next step is to take a better look at our life as we presently know it.

To live an examined life is to be aware. Others would say it's to lift the veil of forgetfulness. An examined life may help us to come to know our soul's journey or the script that we followed to show up here in the first place. An examined life may be the way to the great "unlearning" of those things our domestication—society, education, religion—imposed on us. To know one's Self is to "know."

A Day Together

Let's try to spend a day together—a day in the life of an awakening mind, of one who is just beginning to be aware that all is not as it seems. We will attempt to take baby steps; it's a start, and we all have to start somewhere.

Before we begin, I must say to you, "Buyer beware!" Once you start this journey, you may lose your innocence—the innocence *of not knowing.* You are innocent in that you possess knowledge of which you are unaware. And on this journey, you will become aware of what you have known all along. Your innocence will be gone.

Once you begin to open your mind to what you do in fact already know, you cannot go back to *not* knowing. As you begin this journey—the journey of an examined life, you begin to free yourself from the prison of your own mind. Everything that is happening around you is in your mind; it can't be anywhere else. Without your mind, *are* you? Yes, you have a brain, but your brain is not your mind. You have a body, but without the mind, the body does not function as it should. And consider this: if God is in your mind, *are you therefore in the mind of God?* Then who are we? Who am I? Who are you, and what are we doing here in the first place?

Let's ask!

Chapter 2

Who Are We?

We are spiritual beings having a human experience.
— Teillard de Chardin

Let's begin this journey in which we see with "new eyes."

In the morning as you awaken from your restful sleep, you may find, as many of us do, that you still feel overwhelmed with tiredness. Our daily busy-ness consumes us, and we collectively suffer from exhaustion. It's time to take a moment to catch our breath and to ask our Self why we are here in the first place and what we're supposed to be doing.

But how do I ask? *What* do I ask? Please understand that there is no right or wrong way to ask, but I would suggest that we try to keep it simple. Many of us find ourselves locked into the illusion of time constraints, so let's make this work for us without feeling that we have to fit one more thing into our already over-scheduled day.

Breathing—a Key

If you can, stay in bed for a moment—you don't need to get up; just lie there and become aware of your breathing. Feel it coming into your nostrils; you may notice that it is slightly cool. When you breathe out, your breath is slightly warmed. Give it a try. It's subtle and "delicate" but it's there.

Become a little more aware of your breathing. When you wake up, you are going to be breathing, so it's not that I am asking you to do anything new or different. If you are not breathing, you have a serious problem and no longer need the *space suit* to participate in this movie, and definitely will not need to read this book in order to find your road map home; you have already graduated and moved on to *another* movie.

We'll assume that you *are* breathing—so take a few more breaths. Feel the *Prahna, Chi* (pronounced *Chee*) or Essence, sexy terms for our life force, coming and going from your body. We take breathing for granted because it is what we do unconsciously. When you become aware of this source of life

5

coursing through your body, pay attention to it for a few moments. Paying attention to it will lower your heart rate, calm your mind, and do all kinds of other weird and wonderful things for you. Take a few more moments to feel this life force traveling down into your fingertips and now down into your toes. With your next breath, clear your head. Now take the next breath deep down into your belly. Feel your chest expanding and your shoulders relaxing. If you find that you are breathing in a shallow manner, meaning you are *not* taking it deep into your belly, make a conscious effort to expand your chest and fill your body right down to your groin, right into your reproductive area. It will feel so good that you may want to spend a few moments just observing your breathing and how it feels coming and going from your body. That part of your body may begin to feel more alive. That's good—at least *something* is working!

Make a conscious effort to check your breathing and how you hold your body. Many of us breathe too quickly, our breaths quite shallow. Some have discovered the art of slow deep breathing.

Dealing with Tension

Check to see whether your body is tense or relaxed. If you are not sure, tighten everything up, everything—even screw your face tightly and then let it go. You will notice the difference. An important tip: pay attention during the day and scan your body with your breath. How loose are your shoulders and hands? If they're tight, loosen them up. The best way is to tense everything— every muscle group—as tightly as you can, and then to let the tension go. Notice what tension feels like, and how its absence feels. Especially check your shoulders, chest, neck, and hands. We're often unaware of how tightly we hold our bodies, and wonder why we are so exhausted at the end of the day and why everything hurts.

When we wake up in the morning, we may feel that a runaway truck came through our bedroom in the night and ran over us. We may wake up more exhausted and tired than when we went to bed. What's wrong with this picture? Sleep is supposed to be restful. Some of us suffer from one form of chronic sleep disorder or another and never feel totally rested. We can't seem to get caught up no matter how many hours we spend in bed. Perhaps it's time to get reacquainted with our bodies, our funny little space suits in which we find ourselves trapped.

Try to visualize your breath coming in from the top of your head—the soft spot that you had as a baby—and then let it travel all the way down your spine as you breathe out. Do that a few times and begin to be aware of your spine and the energy that lies trapped there. This breathing will free it up and actually loosen your spine. Become aware of *the life force*, the energy, as it radiates throughout your body.

Feels good, doesn't it! If you stay focused on your breathing for a few moments, it may even feel better. We have *monkeys* running all over our brain; our thoughts are out of control. Slowing them down, harnessing them, or even trying to ignore them for a few moments is not easy. Go back to your breathing and stay aware of it for a few more breaths.

We breathe to stay alive and we take our Breath of Life, our *Prahna*, our Life Force for granted. Taking a moment or two just to be aware will clear your head and energize your body. Enjoy! You can do this at your desk, when you are waiting in traffic, anywhere—it will feel good and reenergize as well as relax you. Hopefully it can easily become a daily ritual, and if in the morning you forget to indulge yourself, to be *nice* to yourself, remember, you can start your day anytime. Just begin to notice and to be aware; stop for a moment to focus on your breathing. Don't force anything; don't do anything unnatural; just be mindful. Take the time to enjoy some deep *aware* breaths. Now, allow your body to find its own natural rhythm. You may be aware of energy points or *chakra* vibrations, colors, or feelings. You may want to focus your eyes inward towards the middle of your forehead, the area we call the "third eye" or "ajna" center. You may want to focus on the energy coming and going from your heart. Take a moment to offer gratitude to this incredible instrument, your heart that works so hard at keeping your space suit working. You may just want to bathe in the love that you become aware of that surrounds you all the time. It is never *not* present. Many of us turn ourselves off, close ourselves down, and refuse this incredible gift that is always present. But play with this for a few minutes. Enjoy the awareness of the energy that moves throughout your body, and feel how it awakens those oftentimes neglected, forgotten parts. You may feel absolutely nothing. It is quite strange how disconnected we've become from our own bodies; it may even be the norm for today.

Perhaps you're feeling that this is a lot of rubbish, and you're not interested in giving yourself this *nice*, simple gift of reconnecting with self at this time. I am asking you to please be patient and to keep trying. You will become aware. If nothing else, you will energize and will feel better in the morning. We all want to feel better in the morning, so we do have a lot to gain by practicing this little ritual.

Like anything else; it may just take some practice. When you were a kid and wanted desperately to ride a bicycle or to learn to skate, dance, sing, or swim, it took a few awkward tries before you found yourself sailing along, but it eventually became second nature to you. After a few attempts, whenever you got on your bike or laced up your skates, it just happened. You didn't even have to give it any thought. Riding your bicycle or skating or whatever your sport of choice was, became second nature. For some it was no effort; it just came naturally. For others, it took a little longer to get in the rhythm and to get that mind/body connection happening. It's worth a little practice, so don't give up on yourself. Be "nice." It works. Now ask.

Asking

Who walks with me? God, Goddess, Allah, Jesus, Cosmic Bob or Cosmic Betty, Jehovah, Higher Power, Creator, Buddha, Hu, Angels, Grandmother, "spam," whatever name you're comfortable with. Names, words, are only symbols of symbols—of something that is beyond what our little minds can understand, so don't get hung up on what you want to call that source of help. Invent a name if need be, or use no name. Use whatever method is comfortable or familiar and non-threatening to you.

Be still. Now ask. "Where do you want me to go, what do you want me to do, what do you want me to say, and to whom?"

There you did it! That wasn't too hard. We are so well trained to be strong, to be independent, to do it ourselves, that reaching out and asking can be a big deal.

The next question is, "How am I going to hear the answer?" How will I know that the universe is speaking to me, that "Cosmic Bob" is actually listening? That there really is *something* out there just waiting for me to ask? And that that *something* will guide me to do what is right for me? That *the Voice* is not just my ego leading me down the proverbial garden path, telling me what I want to hear or not hear? How do I know that I am not just talking to myself and answering my own questions?

I am going to use the word *God*. I know it is not politically correct, but again it's only a word, a symbol for something that defies definition.

We get hung up with words. We try to define a thing, and when we *de*fine it, we *con*fine it. What we're talking about here is an energy force within us, around us, everywhere, always present, always there. We often try to define and confine what we do not understand. And modern science and the new physics is helping us see that there's far more that we don't understand than we had ever dreamed.

The New Physics and God

It is interesting that today, in our present linear time, as science progresses through the new physics, through quantum mechanics, it is beginning to scientifically understand that a universal Life force does exist—one that society refers to variously as Creator, God, Life, Allah, or whomever or whatever. These scientists are not religious leaders. They are not theologians or philosophers or New Thought writers. They are hardcore scientists, physicists, and mathematicians talking about a Universal Energy that permeates All That Is. This is not a new phenomena. Philosophers, scientists, and writers have been alluding to this for thousands of years, and now we have proof—there *is* something within us and around us that fills the universe that we know. That also fills universes far beyond our imagination—that just Is. That just Is, is *all* that there Is. It is within us, around us, right here, right now. "I Am" ALL THAT IS, and ALL THAT IS is within me. Simple, but very complex as we try to "intellectualize" it all.

Blaise Pascal, seventeenth century philosopher, mathematician, scientist, and theologian, in his writings *Pensees*—or *Thoughts*—argues that "reason is by itself inadequate for man's spiritual needs and cannot bring man to God, who can be known only through mystic understanding."

And Martin Buber, who died in 1965, said something further that may interest you. Buber—a German-Israeli philosopher who was a major force in twentieth century Jewish thought and philosophy—in his writings, *I and Thou,* held that God and man can have a direct and mutual "dialogue."

If what I'm saying here sets up an aversion, a fear, some negativity, you may want to ask why. Could it be that you feel you are so special, so separate, that you are *not* a part of ALL THAT IS? Do you think that ALL THAT IS is *not* within you, and that it is *not* you? Or perhaps you feel that the Life Force is in some people, but not in you?

Words as Symbols

Words are symbols. Words sometimes, but not always, give us the ability to communicate. Many philosophic problems we have today are caused by linguistic confusion. When we were infants without words, body language and sound were the primary influences on our simple thoughts. Body language and projected feelings impacted us and molded our feelings about ourselves into the feelings that we have today. Not the words so much as the energy surrounding the words, the feelings and body language that came with the words. Some of us were more sensitive to our circumstances and our perceptions, correct or distorted, and our early domestication created us as we are now. Religion and spiritual beliefs have often been misshapen by linguistic confusion, fears, and projections. Many of the ancient writings, translations, and teachings were influenced by the writers' own personal perceptions based on their world as they knew it. These ancient perceptions still greatly influence our thoughts and belief systems today—oftentimes blinding us to our own truth. They become our personal beliefs, beliefs that define our world.

The Creative Power of Thought

Our thoughts and feelings create emotions, and these emotions create our movie, our illusion, or what you and I call "my life." So if we are lying in bed, feeling pretty depressed about the day that lies ahead of us, that's the day *that we are projecting*. It is our mind that creates our life. Since the beginning of man's search for self, it has been written: "As within, so without," "As above, so below," or simply put "How you feel inside is how your life is outside."

We do not condone insane behavior, but we do condone our insane thoughts. We may believe that we are responsible for what we do, but not for what we think. The truth is that we *are* responsible for what we think, because it is only at this level that we can exercise choice. What we do comes from what we think.

We are much too tolerant of our own mind's wandering, and we passively condone its misbegotten designs. The mind is very powerful, and it never loses its creative force. It never sleeps. Every instant, it is creating.

It is hard to realize that thought and beliefs combine into a power surge that can literally move mountains. We prefer to believe that our thoughts cannot exert real influence. If we believe that what we think is ineffectual, we may want to take a good look at our own lives and at the world we live in.

There are no idle thoughts. All thinking produces form at some level. The universes that the new physics is beginning to discover may be creations of our thoughts, our beliefs, our minds. This again is not a new theory, but if it is fact, it's certainly one huge responsibility!

Doctor Edward De Bono, the man who coined the term "lateral thinking"—said: "The quality of our thinking, will determine the quality or our future." It just may be that it is 'we' who create the future we are about to have.

Freedom of Choice—Blessing or Curse?

It is said that we humans are blessed with free choice. I often think that this is more a curse than a blessing. Jean Paul Sartre, a French philosopher and novelist, held that man is "condemned to be free" and to bear the responsibility of making free choices.

In the creation of our lives, we must give more thought to what we choose to think, act upon, and react to. We act and think as though our actions and thoughts will not affect everything and everyone around us. But the basic law of cause and effect; the most fundamental law there is, says differently. It says that what we believe collectively affects all of us. We are the ingredients of the soup we all find ourselves in. We do not guard our thoughts carefully enough, and for this reason, the world we find ourselves living in is a fear-based world, and is therefore in desperate chaos. It may be time to *stir* the pot and find out what is not working and perhaps add something to make it a little more tasteful.

But this begs the question: "Do we really have free choice, or is this just fate or predestination that we are locked into?" Are we addicted to choosing from fear instead of from love? Are we mindless and choosing from ego instead of from spirit? Is our fate or destiny set, and am I kidding myself that I can run my own show, create my own life, have the life I have always dreamed of having, and in the process change the world around me?

Making Our Lives Different

If we find ourselves in a life that does not complete or complement us, a life that is not joyful, how can we make it different?

I believe that there must first be a readiness, a willingness to "do it different." But readiness is not accomplishment; it is only the *prerequisite* for accomplishment—the two should not be confused. When a state of readiness occurs, by very definition, there is a desire to accomplish. The state of readiness is a potential for a change of mind.

Readiness is also the beginning of confidence. Confidence cannot develop fully until we have a degree of mastery. Whether an enormous amount of time is necessary between readiness and the mastery of controlling your mind is up to you. It is hard to let go of what is familiar, even when it is killing us and keeping us locked in our pain and fear. Once we are awake to our fear thoughts, we understand that the only alternative to these is love. I will address this later and hopefully offer some useful and practical tools to assist in mastering the "monkey minds" that so often run our show.

In the scenario we've created, this is still early morning, and you are lying undisturbed in bed. Now you have asked, "What will you have me do, where will you have me go, what will you have me say, and to whom?" (Sincerity—truly meaning this—will come with practice.) Now it is time to hand it over, to let it go, to say, "Take it away, Cosmic Betty."

You no longer need carry those worrisome thoughts around with you when you get out of bed, those thoughts that keep you a prisoner of your own mind. If you find your mind racing around trying to control situations and orchestrate things, putting them in motion the way it thinks it should, be quiet for a few more moments, reclaim control, just be still and focus on your breathing.

As you lie in bed, you may be thinking about a meeting later in the day that will impact the rest of your life. You may be in incredible pain, or your child is sick, on drugs, out all night, or your spouse or lover has left you. You may be wondering how you are going to make your rent or mortgage, how you are going to feed your family, how they will react when you tell them you are gay or getting divorced. You may have discovered that you have a life-threatening disease.

Whatever your circumstances, you are not alone, not abandoned, not special. Wilhelm Leibniz, a seventeenth century German philosopher, diplomat, and mathematician, was one of the great minds of all time. Along with Sir Isaac Newton, Leibniz was an inventor of calculus and a forefather of modern mathematical logic. He also held that the entire universe is one large system expressing God's plan. If Leibniz was right, you are part of this plan, and therefore part of this incredible life force. Since you are in the image of the Creator/God, you are part of the whole.

You may not have taken time to ask God what the plan is. Or perhaps you have, but have not been quiet enough to hear the answer. When you have quieted and asked, it will be up to you whether you embrace this or some other plan.

The problem is that there are so very many plans, all leading to the same result. We often choose paths that are worrisome and tragic. It need not be so difficult or painful or as complicated as we often make it. One thing we must remember: we are deeply, deeply loved, and have always been loved no matter what—at all times—even if we do not feel it.

But the blinders and thick ear plugs your beliefs have created may keep you from seeing that you are loved. These beliefs may isolate you, remove you, tune you out from this life force that offers only love and a clear sense of direction. They may have put you out on this huge ocean in your little boat with no paddle with which to make it back to shore, and the waves keep on taking you farther and farther out. But now it's time to come home, and I'm handing you a paddle. Life was not intended to be so miserable, so lonely, and so bloody difficult.

Our Naysaying Minds

You may find that your mind often seems to work overtime bringing back memories of everything that happened yesterday, twenty years ago, or everything that you think may happen today or tomorrow or next year, so that it can say, "I told you so." "See it's just like I said it would be."

The interesting thing is, it will probably be exactly so, because that's what you're projecting. So … get *out* of your mind. Those worries and concerns only do you harm. You cannot change anything by worrying about them. Many of us are addicted to worry to such a degree that we cannot even have a conversation unless it's centered in all the terrible things that we perceive around us or in those things we project. Give yourself a break! Let's do some damage control here!

A Philosopher to the Rescue

George Berkeley, (1685-1753) was an Irish philosopher and an Anglican bishop. He believed that everything that exists is dependent on being perceived by a mind. According to this view, material objects are simply collections of "ideas" in the mind of a person or of God. (No, I am *not* making this up, and it is still a widely discussed concept.) Those thoughts, those things, those circumstances, those feelings are not happening now, *except* in your mind. You are making them real in your movie. If we are in this movie together, we can only work on one mind at a time, and that is our own—the only one we have access to.

So be present for a moment. Right here, right now! That is all there is. As you become more mindful, every time your mind takes you back into your negative thoughts and feelings, whenever it goes back into "fear" thoughts, focus on your breathing. It's amazing how, when you focus on your breathing and keep your focus there, your mind will clear. Try that in the middle of a shouting match based around fear. It's pretty hard to be angry or fearful as you focus on your breathing.

Once more, this that I'm telling you is nothing new. So how can you get out of your mind? How can you escape your thoughts, your painful memories, your worries about what may come or not? I am not suggesting that you stick your head in the sand or adopt a Pollyanna complex, but that you make an attempt to become more present and to become more aware of where your mind/thoughts take you.

How can you create a life of peace, a life where there is more than enough, a life that fills you with joy and wonder, a life that YOU create, a life where you are actually in control of your choices, one that allows you to live mindfully, to live in completeness? A life that allows your soul to grow in the plan that you chose long before you had consciousness? I am asking that you simply begin a practice of being more present, of becoming more aware of where your mind/thoughts take you.

Please think of this: "If God is in my mind, and I am in the mind of God, then who am I? Where am I"?

Now go back to your breathing. Take a few moments to feel the pulse of the universe beating within you, calling you to follow your soul's rhythm in the dance of your life.

Chapter 3

Creating Our Own Movie

Somewhere on some planet, sometime and somehow,
Your life will reflect your thoughts of your Now.
—Excerpt from *My Law*
Author unknown

If we do not change our direction, we are likely to end
up where we are headed.
—Ancient Chinese proverb

What regulates the body, so we are told, is the brain.

What we tend to forget is that the brain is not the mind. Remember that having a brain does not mean that one's body works. People in deep comas sometimes regain consciousness and report that they could hear and were aware, but could not communicate or get their body to perform in any way. Clients who have had near death experiences or who had been in a coma were clear and accurate about their observations. They described how they hovered above their bodies, observing, witnessing. They were not in their bodies nor were they able to get them to work, but they were in their minds. After being resuscitated or awakening from their coma, they could clearly account as to what was going on in the room at the time, as to who was present and accurately repeat conversations that took place by others during their coma.

If you are reading this book, then you have a brain that is working, and you have a *mind* that instructs the brain as to what it is to do. Our personalities, our domestication, our life's circumstances sometimes get in the way and cause us to misperceive life itself and All That Is around us. We, the human species, tend to allow our egos (or call them personalities), to cloud the mind with forgetfulness and limit what we see and understand. It's as though we're behind a veil, or looking into a mirror; we are lost in our own shadow, and we think that our shadow or reflection is what is real.

Though the brain exists to *serve* the mind and reflects the thought that is *within* the mind, it is *not* the mind. We mistakenly think that our body and our brain are who we are. Our ego keeps us locked into the concept that "what you *see* is what you get," but we're only looking into the reflection of our reflection and believing that what we see is what is.

Forgetting Where We Came From

The ego tends to cause a forgetfulness to fall over the mind, making most of us forget where we came from. It has caused us to forget who we are, and why we are here in the first place.

Again, we came from a projection of a thought in the mind. Generally, we believe that there is a world out there, but the world we think is *out*side us, is simply the projection of what is *in*side us. Among other things, we forget that we are not alone. Idea and source have been split off; cause and effect have been split off; and now we believe we are in this world and that it is a pretty scary place. When we turn on the news or read the paper or even walk down our own streets, we sometimes see frightening things. We are trapped in our shadow side, in our projection in what we think we see. We no longer know who or what to trust. We are caught up in the movie of our own making, and we are no longer aware of what is real.

The brain does not differentiate between actually having an experience and merely observing on a movie screen a portrayal designed to make you feel that you are there. The adrenaline rush you get while watching violence and horror is the same whether you are actually there or not. Your body is subjected to these stimuli whether real or observed. You may want to pay attention to what you and your family watches or reads or listens to, because the stimuli and imprint is the same as if the event were real.

But in regard to where we came from, we as a species seem to have total amnesia. We have no recall of our origin, we don't remember why we are here, or that there may be a plan. Some of us haven't given it much thought, nor are we really very interested. We think we have too much on our plate and have neither the time nor the inclination to think about this "stuff." We think that we have to stay with what is *real*.

But maybe, just maybe we should look at what *is* real, and see where it's all coming from. We may want to ask why we are willing to pay so dearly to continue the nonstop reruns of this chaotic and destructive movie we find ourselves trapped in.

Of course the ego is now going to protest loudly; it does not want to relinquish its control over our mindlessness.

We may reason in the following mistaken way: the choices we think we have are real but they have all been created from our mind. They are all illusion, and they are all made-up choices. So we are really not choosing anything real—we are simply choosing one illusion over another. "I prefer," one might say, "this illusion rather than that illusion. There is this illusory problem over here, and there is that illusory solution to it over there."

This is the wrong way to think. The problem is simply that we turned away from the source and turned to the ego. In effect, we bet on the wrong horse. And we are not aware that the horse dropped dead in the starting gate and is going absolutely nowhere. Now we spend all of our time trying to revive this dead horse and get it to take us someplace, and there is no way it can do that because it is neither alive nor real.

Alcoholics Anonymous has a wonderful definition of insanity; they say that it is doing the same thing over and over again and expecting the results to be different. Our little human nature is so stubborn and so insane that we persist in trying to get this dead horse up. And it continues to go absolutely nowhere. We whip and cajole and beat it up and do all kinds of things, and the dead horse doesn't hear or respond. It does absolutely nothing. That is what we do in the world. We don't know what we are doing because we don't know about anything else. It is not the horse that has blinders on, it is we ourselves.

We see what the ego wants us to see. It diverts our attention from the location of the real problem—inside us, in our minds—to supposed forces outside.

I know this sounds a bit esoteric and "out there," but think about it. At least give it some thought, and perhaps start a diary in which you write your observations of how you think and feel. And then look at how your life is. Is it a reflection of your thoughts? Is it joyful and are you at peace? If not, how can you project a different life?

Remember. We have been domesticated, and this domestication reinforces our concept of who we are and are not. The ego tells us that we are not good enough, that we can't do this or that, that we are too tall, too short, too fat, too smart, too stupid, etc. Now don't get me wrong. Ego is a very necessary part of who we are. It allows us to differentiate ourselves from the doorknob. But most of us allow the ego to rule our lives.

To help us understand, I will attempt a simple analogy. Let us say that you own a priceless coach (your body) and you have some fine strong horses to pull this coach (your arms and legs). You find a driver (your personality) and give her directions to get you from point A to point B. You are not too clear about the route, but you hand the reins over nonetheless. The driver gets up in the driver's seat (your mind, and she starts to drive your coach. The drive is monotonous, and the tedious scenery lulls you into a deep sleep. (Life 101). The driver now gets carried away with the power of driving these horses, and there is no one to remind her to stay the course. She takes you down all kinds of strange roads and diversions, sometimes into places where there's grave danger and possible harm, over roads that could destroy your coach. Yet you sleep on. Suddenly there is a strong bump in the road.

Life 101 has presented you with the loss of a job, a cancer scare, a death, a sick child, a toxic relationship, etc. The bump causes you to awaken only to find yourself way off track. You're in a very strange and frightening place. Now you must take control of your hired driver (your personality/ego) and help the driver know her place. You remember that you are not your personality (the hired driver). Personality, from person, which comes from the Latin word *persona*, meaning an actor's mask. This personality—this mask—is only a tool in your mind to assist you on your journey from point A to B. You once more become mindful and reclaim responsibility for yourself. And you remind yourself that you are not your mask, and that you have the ability to respond according to who you *really* are.

Now you can take back the control of your journey. Even though you can relax and enjoy the trip, you are now mindful. You have awakened and are clear as to where you are going, once more in charge of completing your plan, of getting back on your path and arriving at your predetermined destination.

This ego to which we give so much power keeps us locked in negative thoughts and circumstances that have stuck to us since we were born. It has created a belief that we are alone, that we have to do this ourselves, that no one is there to help us. And this is just not true.

Perhaps the only solution to our problems—or what we think are our problems—is simply to return to that choice point in our minds, and make another choice; to choose against the ego, to put your personality, your mask, to one side and go towards the source.

Going toward the Source

To get out of our minds is to take our attention from the world so that we can make another choice. Take our attention from our problems or concerns in the world, from the concerns of our own bodies or other people's bodies, and say: "This is not the problem—the problem is back within my mind. I will look within my mind." Now we can finally look at what we chose, at the price we paid for it, and realize that this was stupid. We finally realize that the horse that we were beating is dead. We have allowed that dead horse to touch and influence every thought we have, everything we do, how we perceive who we are. At this point the choice becomes a mindful choice and now *we can truly choose again*. Now we realize that there is another thought system. There is another presence in our minds. And if we choose that presence, our life will change. What I am attempting to make clear is that we do have a choice. This means that the sphere of activity, the sphere of action is not the body, not the brain, and not the world, but the mind. Once we return to our minds, the right choice will be obvious, and we will be mindful as to how and what we need to choose. And when we become truly mindful of our minds, we will get out of our minds—we will let it go. If I am not my body, if I am not my personality, if I am not my mind, then who am I?

Chapter 4

Changing Our Perceptions through Changing Our Minds

Where, after all, do universal human rights begin? In small places, close to home ... without concerned citizens' action to uphold them close to home, we shall look in vain in the larger word.
—Eleanor Roosevelt

No problem can be solved with the same thinking that created it.
—Albert Einstein

Never doubt that a small group of thoughtful committed citizens can change the world. Indeed it is the only thing that ever has.
—Margaret Mead

You are now about to get on with your day. As you shower, remember that we are part of that small percentage of the world's population who can turn on a tap and have hot and cold water when we need it. We love our hot showers and luxurious baths; we would be at a loss without them. And while you remember that, also pay attention to the politics concerning the privatization of water, and be mindful that what we are dumping into our rivers and streams eventually comes back into our drinking and bathing water as well as into the food we produce and consume.

Are you aware that the governing party in Bolivia sold its water to an international corporation to pay down a World Bank loan? The corporation now owned all the water, whether it fell from the sky or came from the river. The already poor peasants had to pay for the water they used. They could barely afford a pail of water on their meager earnings and were charged heavily if found "stealing" *rain* water. I won't go into all the details and craziness. But a seventeen-year-old organized the peasants, and they overthrew a corrupt government that had sold them out. The young leader and many others lost their lives in this confrontation, but the Bolivians reclaimed the right to their own water.

A committed group of people, mostly teenagers, reclaimed what was rightfully theirs and created change. An awareness of these activities in Bolivia can prevent similar things from happening again. This was not a long time ago—only in the past decade. And it happened while no one was paying attention.

Blessing Those Who Bless Us

Martin Luther King had a great many good things to say about the world. But despite his teaching's enduring power, some of it still falls on deaf ears. Here's one we forget: "Before you finish breakfast this morning, you'll have relied on half the world."

So before you have your breakfast, give some thought to how this food came into your possession. As you do, bless the soil, the rain, the wind, and the sun as well as the seed or animal that played out its life's journey to help nourish your body. The farmer who nurtured the land, the pickers who harvested the crop, those who transported it, and all of those involved in getting the food into your supermarket. Remember the storekeeper, the green grocer, the cashier who took your money, and the person who packed the groceries, and bless them as well.

Now bless yourself for all the energy it took to make this possible, your time, your effort to bring this food to serve and nourish your body and the bodies of those who depend upon you. By *bless,* I mean extend to them your feelings of love and gratitude. Do that—extend them to yourself and to all who took part in this wonderful process.

Guarding against Poison

But before you put these things into your mouth or use them on your body, pay attention to what's in them. Read to see if they have harmful chemicals. Are you exposing yourself or members of your family to the possibility of disease? Do these things contain toxic elements? Check out your dairy products, your cereals, your processed and fast foods, even the juice with added vitamins—do it despite the ads purporting that these products are healthy. Some things you eat and use are by-products of petroleum products with added chemicals and flavoring. It only takes a few moments to read the labels. It's true, of course, that you may pay a bit more for the real thing, but it will pay off in the long run, and you are not supporting the large corporations whose bottom line is making their quarterly projections rather than serving you and your family.

It is being proven every day that you are what you eat. There is an epidemic of obesity, diabetes, cancer, heart problems, respiratory illnesses, allergies, etc. We can prevent most of these by being more mindful of what we put into our mouths or on our skin. Our skin, by the way, is the largest organ of our body. If we can't eat a substance, why are we using it as a cream or cosmetic or wearing it as clothing next to our skin? Our skin absorbs its toxins into our bodies. We have no problem understanding the patch used these days for many medical purposes: as anti smoking aids, hormone replacement, etc., but we fail to think about what our skin absorbs throughout the course of our day and at night while we sleep lathered in creams, wrapped in pajamas made of synthetic materials, lying on artificially scented sheets cleaned with caustic products. We purchase cleaning and washing products loaded with harmful chemicals, subject ourselves and our families to toxic gases that we breathe in daily—right in the "safety" of our own homes—and wear our clothes washed & softened, laden with more harmful chemicals. "But they do smell good." We go on, blissfully unaware of the long-term effects they have on our health and well-being. We wonder why there is such an increase in cancer, asthma, behavioral problems, and allergies.

These toxic products also put a huge dent in our pocketbooks. Household edible products such as baking soda, white vinegar, lemon, lavender & tea tree oil, oil of oregano, etc., can do the job just as well if not better, and they are far safer. These natural products will keep your home clean, healthy, and environmentally friendly. The cost is a fraction of those chemically laced products that may cause the death of a small child as well as many of the chronic illnesses that are so difficult to diagnose today.

Most of us are so tired of being tired; it's this onslaught against our well-being wears us down.

If you become more mindful and look after your body, your vehicle, this space suit that you came in, the one that assists you in getting around, it will serve you well. As you put in healthy, high-powered energy food filled with natural nutrients, you make it more fuel-efficient. Your body will run smooth and trouble free. And it will give you years of good service without always being in the repair shop to be serviced. Many of us are more mindful and take better care of our cars then we do of our bodies.

Even many of our bodies themselves are also toxic. Most of us are too acidic. Cancer, the common cold, the flu, thrives in an acidic body. Do some research or seek out professional help in bringing your body back to its natural alkaline state. Many of our North American doctors have little training in nutrition and environmental diseases, but they are slowly being educated through research and being taught that we truly are what we eat. Where our bodies have been, what we have exposed them to externally and what we put into them, and our general emotional state—all these contribute greatly to chronic as well as fatal diseases we face today.

You may want to check out the benefits and the simplicity of eating live foods 'raw': sprouted foods and foods grown in your own area. Just grabbing an apple or a banana, or even better, some berries and a handful of raw unprocessed nuts and seeds in the morning takes little effort, and your body will love it. Not only is it simple and cost effective, but you will also feel energized and satisfied.

There is no further need for me to lecture on nutrition—there are enough good books and information readily available if you are interested in doing the research. But to grasp the importance of this, remember the words of a great eighteenth century poet and dramatist.

> *Take care of your body with steadfast fidelity. The soul must see through these eyes alone, and if they are dim, the whole world is clouded.*
>
> —Johann Wolfgang von Goethe

Playing Fair

Every time you take your morning cup of coffee, tea, or nibble on a chocolate bar—the one whose calories you promised yourself you'll work off eventually— or when you consume just about anything else, for that matter, chances are you'll be enjoying the fruits of a poor or developing country's labor. This is fine, in theory.

As we consume our food, do we ask whether the farmers, laborers, or factory workers have been fairly paid for their produce or their labor? Has this product been brought to us by large corporations where the bottom line is financial gain and the basic concept is marketability? Most often they don't factor taste and nutrient value into their production.

It's important that we think about these things. All that is done around the globe is done by individuals, and in the long run, affects us as individuals. Also remember that people are the ones who create change; that's me, that's you, we are "the" people who can make it happen.

Again I quote Mr. King; "Before you finish breakfast this morning, you'll have relied on half the world."

This quote is a distillation of the entire Fair Trade movement.

The Fair Trade movement is independent from most charities, and definitely free from corporate influence. The so-called "free trade" or "globalization" being imposed on third world countries is creating major problems. There is a huge difference between free trade, or globalization, and *fair* trade.

Free trade or globalization, as it is practiced today, may be the single biggest threat to the rights of indigenous peoples, or traditional peoples, or peasants, worldwide. To counter this threat, the Fair Trade Foundation seeks to change the basic attitudes—minds—of consumers.

But in despair, you cry out, "I don't have time to research all the products I use and the food I consume. So help me out!" That's what the Fair Trade Foundation seeks to do. It encourages and organizes the distribution of fair trade goods around the world. It is the axis on which all of the food producers and corporations operate their fair trade campaigns, and it has created the universal Fair Trade logo. At present the symbols may vary from country to country but take a moment to inquirer as to what supplier handles Fair Trade products.

What Shall We Eat?

When you are out shopping for groceries, try to buy locally, frequent your local markets, or look for the Fair Trade logo on the packaging. Speak to the store manager about bringing in more Fair Trade products and locally grown produce. I have found that our local stores are more than willing to accommodate demand for more organic, environmentally safe, and labor friendly products as long as consumers continue to buy them. You may pay a little more, but you're getting full value for your money and contributing towards a standard of living for the average indigenous farmer or laborer.

The more we ask even the large corporations for Fair Trade products, the more they will stock them, for they, too, are governed by demand. That's where the consumer comes in. That's you and me; without us they are out of business.

Because of consumer demand, many of our fast food franchises are beginning to sell foods with less sugar and no trans fat. The taste is still there, and the product is now less harmful to your health. Currently, the largest supermarket is Wal-mart, and they are responding to the demand for more organic and Fair Trade products. They are increasing their organic shelf space to accommodate their consumers' demands—the bottom line being more profit—but even this has its downside, because it may be harmful to the local small farmer. Wal-mart's great success is bringing their product in at the lowest price makes it almost impossible for the small organic farmer to survive.

Slow Food is a relatively new organization founded in Italy in 1986 by Carlo Petrini, a former journalist, in response to the opening of a McDonald's outlet in Rome's famous Piazza d' Espagna. He noticed the decline of good quality local foods in his region and decided to do something about it. Slow Food's efforts are aimed at helping recreate a world in which people are interested in, knowledgeable about, and receptive to high quality food. The goal is to revive passion for such food so we will reject the second-rate wares served along our highways and in the fast food courts of shopping malls.

Mr. Petrini has announced to the world, "Pleasure without knowledge is merely self-indulgence."

In other words, when it comes to knowing where our food comes from, we eat with our heads in the sand. This is something the food industry is quick to exploit. The gap between producer and consumer is getting wider by the minute. Slow Food encourages and protects what it sees as outposts of traditional farming and/or production that are under siege from modern, globalized agriculture.

The International Presidia was established as another non-profit foundation to support projects that maintain the biodiversity of our food supply. The organization stresses that an educational organization dedicated to the stewardship of the land and ecologically sound food production is essential to our future. Not to mention that living a slower, more harmonious life is something that will help us all.

This is good for both the body and the soul.

Research is finding that some of the nutrients we try to provide for our bodies through multivitamins and extracted antioxidants may be doing us harm. The body is not able to absorb them as well as we thought, leaving us depleted and our pocketbooks lighter.

We know that the foods today do not contain the nutrient value that they had in the early part of the twentieth century. Our soils and our modern farming techniques have created a nutritional deficiency. Our bodies are starving despite our obesity, and many of us find ourselves very tired by midday.

Through mindfulness regarding your food, you can make it possible for your body to do what it was designed to do. The awakening mind demands that its enjoyment of the pleasures of the table be based on understanding where and how our food is grown.

Having Eaten Well, Now What?

Now that we have become more interested in what we eat, in what we put into our bodies, what do we do with the waste? Recycle the waste, compost as much as you can, and return it back to the soil.

I am impressed to find that many large cities have small companies who will collect your compost if you have no need for it. This is wonderful. For those who live in apartments or who have no interest in or time to garden, a few ingenious folk have created their own business. They collect and turn your garbage into gardening soil, fuel, or other home products. Call around or ask your local environmental group what recycling companies are available in your area. They oftentimes will pick it up right at your door. Become good stewards of your land and your surroundings, and if these services are not available in your community, you might think of starting them yourself.

Pay attention and become mindful. The implications are many and far reaching. It is time we wake up and find out what is going on that may impact our standard of living and leave a bereft planet to our grandchildren's children.

And What Shall We Wear?

Imagine that! You haven't even left the house for work or school, and already you have made great strides in opening up your mind and simplifying your life. But you can't go out the door naked, so what do we do about being mindful when it comes to clothing? "What am I going to put on?" you ask. Our closets are full, but we lament that we've nothing to wear.

Check out some of the wonderful organic natural fibers now being made into fabric; these include woodchips, the diversity of hemp that, while being grown, actually cleans up toxic land, and the ever-renewable bamboo. The designs are getting better; they wash beautifully; they always look fresh and new; and they seem to last forever. There are no harmful chemicals involved, nor has the land been stripped and raped in the process of growing it. And as a bonus, they feel wonderful against your skin!

Of course there are now those great consignment stores to browse and poke around in. There are people who shop the world and bring it to your neighborhood. The items of clothing in these stores have been gently used, and you can recycle them again for someone else to enjoy at a fraction of the original cost. Get involved with a family clothing cooperative, or start one in your neighborhood. There is plenty of information on how to do this successfully. You can be part of a cooperative that not only supplies clothes, food, furniture, household goods, but also deals in car sharing. Whatever you can conceive can be manifested.

If you are like me, you have a closetful of clothes and usually end up wearing the same three or four pieces most of the time. So why do we accumulate all of this *stuff*? The clutter that bogs us down, that confuses us, that takes time to sort through and move around, that takes up more and more space, and eats away at our precious time?

In Tom Robbins' book, *Fierce Invalids Home From Hot Climates,* he put it quite succinctly:

> Things. *Cosas.* Things attach themselves like leeches to the human soul,
> and then they bleed out the sweetness and the music and the primordial

joy of being unencumbered upon the land. *Comprende?* People feel tremendous pressure to settle down in some sort of permanent space and fill it up with stuff, but deep inside, they resent those structures, and they're scared to death of that stuff because they know it controls them and restricts their movements. That's why they relish the boom-boom cinema. On a symbolic level, it annihilates their inanimate wardens and blows away the walls of their various traps.[2]

We buy because the media infiltrates our thinking and promotes the idea that we need the latest whatever. We hide in movies (the boom-boom cinema) or in noisy surroundings with some form of electronic media blasting and numbing our thoughts as we try to escape from our impotency. As we head off to work or our studies, whether we are self-employed, in the service industry, education, health, public service, government, investments, or whatever, we should ask ourselves what role we play in perpetuating the feeling of despair or in plundering Earth and how can we change this grave scenario.

Once more, many of us have the choice between taking a private vehicle, public transport, or are able to get wherever we are going under our own horsepower. What we have is a choice. If you have the opportunity, choose one that serves the good of the whole; you may even *enjoy* the change. If it creates more stress and negativity, don't do it—you are just adding your emotions, your negative feelings, to the collective boiling pot of this planet's wrongs.

Awakening to Our Life Styles

In the Canadian documentary, *The Corporation*[3], Michael Moore commented that both he and his wife and their respective families worked in the automobile industry, and that they had no idea that the work they were doing would be one of the chief contributors to the melting of the polar ice caps. At that time they had neither awareness nor information of the far-reaching implications of our good or bad choices.

Today, with our growing awareness, we are given the opportunity to choose between benefiting or plundering the planet. Many of us work hard and buy the toys we want or think we need: the larger or newer house, the bigger or better car, the latest fashion or electronic device.

But as we awaken, we will look into just how much time and effort we need to put into our work in order to purchase what we think we need and how much damage we may be doing to ourselves and our planet.

Henry Thoreau wrote in 1845: "I went to the woods because I wished to live deliberately, to confront all of the essential facts of life, and see if I could learn what it had to teach, and not, when I came to die, to discover that I had not lived ... I wanted to live deep and suck out all the marrow of life ..."

In Duane Elgin's book, *Voluntary Simplicity*, he says, "there is no special virtue to the phrase voluntary simplicity—it is merely a label, and a somewhat awkward label at that. Still, it does acknowledge explicitly that simpler living integrates both inner and outer aspects of life into an organic and purposeful whole." Mr. Elgin writes that to live more voluntarily is to live more deliberately, intentionally, and purposefully—in short, it is to live more consciously. [4]

We cannot be deliberate when our focus is distracted. We cannot be intentional when we are not paying attention. Many of us live lives that are just a blur; we are not focused. Bombarded with sound bites, information, family and business demands, we have forgotten that this is MY life. We cannot be purposeful when we are not being present. Therefore, to act in a voluntary manner, we must be aware of ourselves. This requires that we not only pay attention to our actions in the outer world, but also that we pay attention to *ourselves acting*—which is to say, our *inner* world. The less we attend to what is happening outside of us and inside of us, the poorer our quality of life.

Duane Elgin writes, "To live simply is to approach life and each moment as inherently worthy of our attention and respect, consciously attending to the small details of life. In attending to these details, we nurture the soul." [5]

Thomas Moore explains in *Care of the Soul*: "Care of the soul requires craft, skill, attention, and art. To live with a high degree of artfulness means to attend to the small things that keep the soul engaged ... To the soul, the most minute details and the most ordinary activities, carried out with mindfulness and art, have an effect far beyond their apparent insignificance."

Who Controls My Lifestyle?

Gene Youngblood, more than twenty years ago, wrote that the mass media could hold back human evolution simply by controlling the perception of alternatives. He said that if we want to perpetuate the status quo, we do not need to convince the public to become addicted consumers; all we must do is prevent genuine desire for any other way of life from being publicly expressed and collectively validated.

"Desire is learned. Desire is cultivated. It's a habit formed through continuous repetition, but we cannot cultivate that which isn't available. We don't order a dish that isn't on the menu. We don't vote for a candidate who isn't on the ballot. What could be a more radical example of totalitarianism than the power of the mass media to synthesize the only politically relevant reality, specifying for most people most of the time what's real and what's not, what's important and what's not? This, I submit, is the very essence of totalitarianism: the control of desire through the control of perception."

The frightening part of Youngblood's statement is that we perpetuate this condition through our mindlessness; we are too tired or lazy to think for ourselves.

Pretty scary stuff—it shows how easily manipulated we are and how vulnerable we are, and how much we need to be accepted, to be a part of the collective consumer consciousness, to have even our beliefs dictated to us. We have not been shown that there are alternatives. We have been told that *ours* is the best way of life.

When Mother Theresa visited North America, she said that North Americans had the worst disease possible, that of loneliness and isolation.

Alternatives

Let's give ourselves permission to look at alternatives that already exist and then create alternatives of our own. We could experience another way of living, another perception of how we want to live life so that we are truly present, truly mindful.

If you saw the movie, *The Last Samurai*, and observed the serenity in the village where the actor Tom Cruise found himself a prisoner, you saw that every movement was spent in mindfulness; every ordinary activity had an art form, a beauty, a serenity, whether stirring the pot, working in the fields, or even walking. There was a clear intent and purpose to every action; everyday living was a mindful meditation. You could feel and experience the peace just by watching the movie.

To live more simply is to live more purposely and with a minimum of needless distraction. This is a very personal insight, and we each have our own concept of how we feel or don't feel. We each know where our lives are unnecessarily complicated—or do we? We are at least all painfully aware of the clutter and pretense that weighs upon us and makes our passage through the world more cumbersome and awkward.

To live more simply is to unburden ourselves, to live more lightly, cleanly, joyfully. It is to establish a more direct, unpretentious, and unencumbered relationship with all aspects of our lives: the things that we consume, the work that we do, our relationships with others, our connections with nature and the cosmos, and more.

In Mr. Elgin's book, he says, "Simplicity of living means meeting life face-to-face. It means confronting life clearly, without unnecessary distractions. It means being direct and honest in relationships of all kinds. It means taking life as it is—straight and unadulterated."

Taking Inventory

Ask yourself: "Am I living up to expectations imposed on me by society, or by my need for other people's acceptance and approval, or am I comfortable in my own skin, doing what fills me and meets my needs? Do I feel trapped? Am I possessed by my possessions? Do I find myself working more, longer hours, too tired, too busy, too caught up in the importance of my work to spend time with my spouse, with my children, with my family and/or friends?"

We often overcompensate and feel we have to be "strong" for everyone else. We buy our children or grandchildren the biggest or the best because we can't give them our time; so, to appease our guilt or to fill some hole in the soul, we buy. It may all *look* good, but if we allow ourselves to take off our masks, to come out of hiding, to come out of our denial, how would we honestly feel about the way we're handling this?

Can we feel our soul calling? Are we full of joy? Do we feel complete, or is there an unease about our lives or life in general?

Chapter 5

Creating Change in our Businesses and Corporations

If you have no peace, it is because we have forgotten that we belong to each other.

—Mother Theresa

It seems to me that one of the most basic human experiences, one that is genuinely universal and unites—or, more precisely, could unite— all of humanity is the experience of transcendence in the broadest sense of the word.

—Vaclav Havel
President, Czech Republic

As you begin your work or study day, whether at home, in a small private office, a learning or teaching institute, a health care facility, or whatever, you are still linked to a large transnational corporation. Think about it. How do you do your banking, your grocery shopping, and what kind of telecommunication system did you use this morning? Where did you buy the clothes you're wearing? What form of transportation did you use, and what brand of coffee are you drinking?

Many of us protest at least somewhat against transnational corporations, politicians, and global organizations that are operating without accountability. We protest against those we regard as causing or exacerbating global warming, ecological destruction, pollution, or the widening gap between rich and poor. We inevitably blame them. Often, we go further, and blame individuals who shop at supermarkets, or who fail to buy Fair Trade or organic foods, and so on. In protesting against them, or in decrying their behaviour, we inevitably point our fingers: "YOU," we say, "are the ones who are destroying our world!" It's not too much of an exaggeration to say that the global justice movement's principal mode of action is protest; a mode that inescapably implies the blaming of one section of society or another, or one institution or another, for our global ills. And to be fair, there's a lot to protest about, and without protest these important issues would never come to wider public attention.

Mea Culpa

But dire as our global problems undoubtedly are, should not we ask whether, in some sense, we are all to blame for our present predicament? "Let he who is without sin cast the first stone …"After all, who amongst us lives so separately from the global economy as to honestly claim not to be contributing in some way to our present problems, be it by driving when we might walk or cycle, by buying the products of transnational corporations when something more eco- or socially friendly might be better, or by failing to buy organic food when cheaper non-organic alternatives better suit our budgets? Otherwise, this becomes only one more battle between *them and us*. We continue to judge those we believe are not living up to our personal criteria for saving the planet.

Each of us plays a part, to a greater or lesser extent, in perpetuating the problem. The planet doesn't look too healthy, and it is our world, and if it's all in our minds, perhaps it's time we begin to live in *mindfulness*—if *only* to save the planet! And if we are part of this great collective consciousness, let's not permit ourselves to be diverted from what should be a common effort to find solutions. Let's not involve ourselves in the battle between *us and them*, an endless loop of blame and counter blame. Like our individual relationships, if we continue with the "I said—He said—She said," kinds of exchanges, nothing gets resolved.

Corporate Helplessness

You don't need to be a rocket scientist to conclude that, in a global market, corporations can generally only afford to behave as responsibly as the aggregate behaviour of their major competitors permits, and, since they cannot reliably count on the group's simultaneously taking on higher standards, it is virtually impossible for one or a restricted number of market players to make the first move. So while it's clear that corporations could take some small steps towards more responsible behaviour and should be encouraged to do so, we shouldn't fool ourselves into thinking that they have the power to make the really substantive and fundamental changes needed to solve our global problems. Indeed, they manifestly don't, and perhaps cannot.

Do we really think that business leaders are any less aware of our environmental crises than anyone else? They live here; they can't miss what is happening around them. Remember, all that is happening, people are the actors, and I personally feel that when given the opportunity to freely be who they are, most people are honorable and loving. Many of them—perhaps most of them—are caught in a vicious circle of destructive global competition that systematically prevents them from behaving in the way activists, and even they themselves, would like.

In his book, *When Corporations Rule the World*, David Korten astutely observed that, "With financial markets demanding maximum short-term gains and corporate raiders standing by to trash any company that isn't externalizing every possible cost, efforts to fix the problem by raising the social consciousness of managers misdefine the problem. There are plenty of socially conscious managers. The problem is a predatory system that makes it difficult for them to survive. This creates a terrible dilemma for managers who have a true social vision of the corporation's role in society. They must either compromise their vision or run a great risk of being expelled by the system."[6]

As the corporate players often point out, "If we don't do it, our competitors will!" and in a globally de-regulated market, they are right. Would we behave in the same way if we were in their corporate shoes? But that does not make it right, so how can we resolve this problem without the warring and the anger and the finger-pointing and the isolation that *them versus us* imposes?

Maybe if we look at the problem without the fear, we will see that it is not the corporations or their CEOs at whom we should be directing our primary fire, but at the destructively competitive global market system of which they are merely the most high-profile prisoners.

The Role of Governments

We are becoming more aware that the only persons we can focus on at this point, the only persons we can change to help resolve this dilemma, are ourselves. We may have to rethink what we invest in, why and how and what we buy. The same applies to creating change in our government. "No problem can be solved with the same thinking that created it," Einstein said. And what about governments; the institutions responsible for having created the system, and our leaders who are charged with regulating markets to balance social and environmental interests with those of business?

In a world where capital and employment quickly move to any country where costs are lower and profits therefore higher, what chance do governments have to impose increased regulations or taxes on business to protect society or the environment? Doing so will only invite employment and investment to move elsewhere. Environmentalists commonly decry government laxity in properly regulating corporations, but what choice do governments have when they cannot count on *other governments* doing likewise? Any government that makes significant moves to tighten environmental or social protection regulations faces capital flight, a loss of jobs, of its nation losing the ability to compete, and a resulting loss of votes. Again, that's not to say that governments are powerless to do anything at all to improve matters or that we should stop pressuring them. But it does mean that their room for maneuver is curtailed to the point where they, too, are largely caught in the same vicious circle as everyone else.

The Tsunami in the Far East and the devastation of New Orleans made it quite clear that the infrastructures necessary for those regions to take care of their own were not in place in either that third world country or in the United States of America. The "system" in one of the most advanced countries in the world did not work. Neither was there a system that worked in the Far East. Individual human beings from various parts of the world came forward on their own dime and said, "How can I help?" The world had never seen such an outpouring of generosity and true feeling of community. Once again, a reminder that it's all done by people—people like you and me. And when these things occur, change happens.

The same applies to the crises in Europe. At the heart of the European standoff is what everyone in France and Germany will tell you is a division between "the social-Europe," (meaning the system of social democratic spending programs that have made life, even for the very poor, so much better in western Europe than anywhere else in the world), and "American style liberalism" or "Anglo-American capitalism"—the key word there being "American"—and the *idea* that in the American system, business will be able to do largely as it pleases. The adoption of the American style was to allow corporations in all twenty-five European countries to operate within each other's borders as if they were at home. This would allow each country to be less generous than the other in order to create greater profits for corporations within their borders.

Twenty or so years ago in Canada, debates pitted "the global market" against "Canada's social-safety net." Strangely, Canada today manages to have good amounts of both, and it seems to accept that more of the former lets us have more of the latter. The Canadian people became involved and their voices were heard.

In northern Europe, home to the fairest and most economically successful societies in the world, it is widely understood that a nation needs to create good conditions for competitive business in order to drum up wealth that can then be redistributed in huge doses to the poor. Just take a look at what Ireland has been able to do in the last few decades. Ireland is one of the wealthiest and most successful countries in Europe. The people of Ireland wanted to take responsibility for their own well-being. Years of division, strife and bloodshed were no longer acceptable. Ordinary people got involved in creating a truce, a time of peace. The economy followed, and social justice is now well entrenched.

At one point in my life, I had great political aspirations. I ran for a national political party that had been in power for a long time, and in that election, we were voted out of office. It was not a vote for the other major party, but a vote against the present sitting government. The people I met as I campaigned touched me with their openness and honesty, and they believed that the present government was neither listening nor representing their best interests.

They were saying, "We want a cleaner and safer world, good education for our children, a medical program that is available to everyone. We want to believe that we have the freedom to make a living and to own property and to trust that there is a safety net within our system that will not leave us destitute. We want good leadership that we can trust and pride in our country. We want to be good stewards of our planet and care for one another. We want to live in peace."

Today, decades later, these same wants exist, but is anyone really listening, and, given our present situation, can anyone really create these changes?

Spiritual Activism

Margaret Mead's ageless message has a way of playing over and over in my head:

> Never doubt that a small group of thoughtful, committed citizens can change the world. Indeed it is the only thing that ever has.

With these words as my mantra, I put my political aspirations aside and put into practice what I had been teaching and mentoring for years; I became a "spiritual activist," which simply meant to me to "do what comes next with joy and with integrity." So what came next for me was the concept that our country should have a Department of Peace and a minister of peace who would report directly to the prime minister. If we could initiate it in Canada, a country that is the very epitome of peacekeeping, then other countries would follow. No country wants to be seen to be against peace.

In time, maybe not in my time, but in my grandchildren's children's time, when the idea of waging war is no longer acceptable, the world's ministers of peace will be engaged in waging peace. Not by acts of aggression, but by acts of forgiveness, monitoring, and understanding.

Our Universal Desire—and Disappointment

Every citizen wants peace; our governments are made up of citizens; we just have not reached an awareness of how to put it into our international context. Our nation is in the process of maturing, and so are other nations. We are hopefully leaving behind our rebellious, narcissistic stance, and are reaching a point in which we will come together as a community of nations. The phrase, *one person at a time*, reminds us that nations are made up of people. So perhaps the only way for us to start is to create change in our own backyards.

I thought it would be simple matter, gathering like-minded people to create a grassroots organization that would tell our sitting prime minister that the people of Canada wanted a Federal Department of Peace and a minister of peace to represent a "Voice of Peace" in the House of Commons. But it did not turn out to be so. The US, the UK, and New Zealand have also initiated campaigns for departments of peace in their respective countries. Some of the initial colleagues on my team became disheartened and left, believing that we were wasting our time. One of the members sent me an email listing all the reasons why it would not work. This was my answer.

> Dear Vincent:
>
> You have asked a very metaphysical question. Yes, you are right, a Department of Peace will not bring peace, but it is a start. Woman's right to vote did not immediately bring equality, but it was a start, and a couple of decades later, look where we are. It's not perfect, but change is happening.
>
> A Department of Health does not make everyone healthy, but after many decades, ours is slowly making the masses aware of prevention through education so that we have become more responsible for our own quality of life. I could go on and on about taking one small step to create change, but let's look at your question—War! Acts of aggression based on "scarcity" have been around forever; even our animal kingdoms wage war over territory and food sources.
>
> We here in the Western world see ourselves as innocent; we hold grievances. We look to others for answers to resolve our problems. We demand change of everyone except ourselves. We maintain that if someone other than we spoke or acted differently, we would have a different world. Our lives would be better. It doesn't work that way. We see the world as being full of oppressors (the usual targets of political activism), and claim this as justification for our own attacks on the world. We say we are waging peace, and we wear a "face of innocence," perceiving ourselves as different from the others.
>
> Our "face of innocence" is intended to show others—and ourselves—that we are good persons in an evil world. A world that makes us angry and fearful, one that is wicked and unable to provide

us with the love and shelter that our innocence deserves. But *each* faction believes that it is good within an evil world. Each faction sees its members as innocent, and those who oppose them as guilty oppressors.

Political action is one way in which we can attempt to reach out to others. If we can approach this problem with clear intent and a clear purpose and not with a warring mind, but with a mind that holds peace, we will ultimately bring about real, positive change (because such an approach communicates a real change of mind) no matter what its outward form is; a Department of Peace, a Peace University, a Coalition for Peace, etc.

Jesus of Nazareth, Gottama the Buddha, Gandhi, and Martin Luther King, John Doe, and many, many others have contributed toward transforming the world. Despite some quirky personality traits, their actions stemmed from minds that were incredibly loving and forgiving. I believe that the love and forgiveness they exemplified was the real source of their power as they took their stands in the world. So, if you feel motivated to take political action, do so only because it gives you peace, is joyful, and fills you. If your own internal guidance brings you to it, then by all means, act, but may I offer a few suggestions? Observe your mind as you act; be on the lookout for the egotistic motivations, and practice mental vigilance. Be clear as to your intent and purpose and build upon it. We don't condone insane behaviour in others, but we condone our own insane thoughts, and it is our thoughts that create the chaos we are in.

This is a pretty grim picture, and I don't want to overstate the case. Certainly there are genuinely loving political activists as there are genuinely loving politicians. It is quite possible to participate politically in a genuinely loving way. But it is my impression that political and social justice movements are motivated, at least in part, by a desire to attack and punish the "oppressors," whoever those "oppressors" may be. Seek not to change the world, but choose to change your mind about the world. We usually focus on changing externals because there is something that wants to distract us from the crucial business of changing our minds. Rather than focusing on all those guilty oppressors out there, our focus should always be on healing our own perception of the world. War in the physical world comes from ideas and feelings that exist in the world of the mind. To have peace, we must change the mind. And the only way to change one's mind is to educate, educate, and educate. The Department of Peace is simply an umbrella where all peace related activities can have their say and be represented in one way or another.

It is only a beginning, but it is a beginning that could lead to your grandchildren's children living in a time when peace is a normal state around the world. Hopefully, a Department of Peace would eventually have the resources to train more peacekeepers, the resources to send emissaries and diplomats, the resources to set up schools and training centers, to educate, educate, and educate.

South Korea has a University of Peace. Costa Rica has a University of Peace; thus two small countries have launched a new way of being. There is a movement in the U.S. to have a university of peace in every state. Over time, peace will become a way of life the same as, over time, we have become aware that war is no longer the answer; so, as John Lennon so aptly put it "Give (the department of) Peace a chance."

Sandra

All in the Same Boat

Activists should ask themselves whether they would act differently if, instead of our politicians, they themselves were sitting in government. When significant strides toward protecting society or the environment mean losing jobs and votes, would we really behave much differently than the politicians we so commonly decry?

By blaming governments or corporations or international institutions, we actually accord them far more credit than they really deserve. For in blaming them and in holding them responsible, we imply that they have the power to substantially change the system.

We should instead recognize that the lunatic herd mentality of global markets has already taken over the asylum. Surely, therefore, the greatest mistake we can make in our fight for global justice is to blame others for our sorry global predicament. Blaming others implies that we ourselves are blameless, or that we could do better, all the while failing to recognize that we are all to blame, and that we ourselves would likely behave in much the same way as those we presently vilify. In so doing, we perpetuate division, discord, and resentment; we build adversarial barriers instead of removing them, and we thus make impossible the atmosphere of cooperation, understanding, and forgiveness needed to foster an atmosphere of global community— an atmosphere in which the productive negotiations necessary to finding appropriate solutions could evolve.

When, finally, we take all this on board, far from being overcome by feelings of desperation and despair, we will paradoxically reach a crucial and fundamentally important intellectual and spiritual turning point—a point at which we can move on to a new and liberating level in our thinking and being. We move from what the prominent American philosopher Ken Wilber calls "first tier" thinking to "second tier" thinking; from nation-centric thinking to world-centric thinking; from what he calls "flatland reductionism" to integral holism.

Once we stop blaming others, we start to see that, in reality, no single person, group, organization, country, religion, or culture can be singled out. We start to see that even those who benefit hugely from the status quo are in no position to actually change the system, and we start to see that we are all caught, to a greater or lesser extent, in the vicious circle of globally destructive competition: a *prisoner's dilemma* from which there is, ordinarily, no way out. In short, we start to see, finally, that we are all in the same boat.

A Collective Realization

Such a collective realization as this would take us a long way toward creating the pre-conditions for building a genuine global community, toward the conditions of forgiveness and non-judgemental acceptance of ourselves and each other, toward the inclusiveness necessary to beginning our collaborative search for global solutions. After all, it is upon such a state of genuine global community that any properly functioning global democracy must surely depend.

In short, we would have created the conditions in which we could recognize the reality that we are ALL ONE; all one in the recognition of our common human fallibility and brokenness, all one in the celebration of each other's different-ness, all one in the brotherhood and sisterhood of humanity, and all one in the eye of our respective god.

I would like to reinforce what Einstein in his great wisdom put very simply, "No problem can be solved with the same thinking that created it."

So what are we thinking? Do we really understand that our thoughts do count? That yours, mine, and ours make up the global consciousness? Once more, it's all about us, even though we may want to keep out of it, separate and apart. Unfortunately, we can not remain apart. We can no longer just be an observer. We can no longer stay uninvolved; this is about you, me, and us. You are in this world as much as I am. We are part of this collective dream.

A Single, Reasoning Organism

Hegel, (1770-1831) the great German philosopher, based his beliefs on his concept of the world as a single organism that is developing by its own inner logic. As we go through various stages, we eventually come to embody reason. Since we inhabit and cohabit in this world as a unit called the human species, as we begin to embody reason, as we educate ourselves through an awareness of who we are, we as a single humanoid, begin to have an affect on the collective and change our reality.

The world is a single organism, and we are IT. As our dream becomes more lucid, more controllable, and as we truly see ourselves for the first time, we change the world for the better. Again, I am not making this up. I'm not writing about something new; the same things have been said for millennia. Maybe as I put it in a slightly different linguistic pattern, we can acknowledge what we already know.

Parmenides, not a French philosopher this time, but a man who lived before Socrates, held that "being" is the basic substance and ultimate reality of which all things are composed, and that motion, change, time, difference, and reality are illusions of the senses.

So how does one become a human *being* and begin to *see* through those new eyes with clarity and mindfulness?

Chapter 6

Creating Change through Our Media

You may say that I'm a dreamer
But I'm not the only one.

—from "Imagine"
By John Lennon

In John Lennon's song "Imagine," he asks us to join him so that the world can recognize that we are all in this dream together.

I admit that I too am a dreamer, and I really do believe most of us are. I can't say that I have met anyone who does not dream of "peace on earth, good will to man." We are aware that this world we live in, this planet Earth, is the only one in our solar system (that we presently know of) that will support us as a species. We also know that there are dead zones in our oceans, contaminated soil, toxic air, and polluted water. Most governments and scientists are now admitting that humans are responsible for the severity of climate change.

The World Wildlife Fund, an independent organization that turns up every couple of years with its *Living Planet Report*, has grown increasingly concerned about Earth's capacity to sustain life when rising populations refuse to curb their appetites. By the WWF's measure, since the 1980s, we have been consuming Earth's resources faster than Earth can produce them and faster than it can absorb the results. A moderate, business-as-usual calculation based on the "slow, steady growth of economies and populations," indicates that by 2050, humans will demand of nature twice what nature can provide. It's a striking image, that at the current rate, humanity will need two planets' worth of resources to do in 2050 what it was doing in the 1980s.

Such ecological warnings come so often that they risk being treated as background noise: "The world's in danger, yada yada." But as the effort to combat global warming shows, the world is waking up. We are being reminded that the planetary emission of carbon dioxide from the burning of fossil fuels was eight times higher in 2003 than in 1961. Individuals are beginning to want to curb their excesses and are looking for energy efficiency, and with this change in the attitudes of people, governments may have greater resolve to send the right price signals to encourage conservation.

Images are compelling, and the mental picture of our soon needing two planets remains striking. Presently we've just got the one at our disposal.

The Role of Media

Imagine television and the written media airing regular programs telling the good news around the world—programs that amplify the actions of the millions of wonderful people who are already actually making a huge contribution towards healing this planet. Would that not give us hope and the desire to be part of this movement of change? Would we not want to be part of the solution instead of part of the problem?

Imagine on-going television programming giving witness to the wonderful deeds and heroic acts of individuals, communities, and organizations where kindness and love are reinforced.

This would bring real change; our children would see this as the norm and would act accordingly. Our teenagers who are healthily trying to push the boundaries would have a viable outlet into which they might channel their energy and their creativity.

One example is Oprah Winfrey and her contribution. Oprah came from very humble and troubled roots. She answered "the call" and shares her love for humanity by bringing (extra) ordinary people into our homes. Many of those people are reflections of ourselves We can relate to their lives, to the healing that is taking place, and we are drawn to emulate them. They make us aware of the work they do as they recognize the divine in themselves and in others, and we see how they are changing the world one person at a time. Ordinary people have become very *extra*ordinary, and some media programming offers us an opportunity to recognize this. But that is not the norm—yet.

A few years ago *60 Minutes*, aired a show called "Hope Meadows." It featured a ten-year-old "throwaway" boy from Harlem. He said: "When I came to live in Hope Meadows, all I knew was how to be bad. I was failing everything at school. I didn't want to go to no school. Now all I want to do is be good. I have really good grades now. I have so many grandmothers and grandfathers and a family that loves me, and I have a home where I'm safe. I know that they all love me, and I am going to be the best I can be."

I was deeply moved and grateful for the enlightened bureaucrats who allowed that to happen, bless them. Hopefully the airing of this program touched the lives of others who see that they can in their own way recreate similar communities of love and caring for our lost children. Hope Meadows is not in some third world country; it's right here in North America. And right here in North America is where the change needs to happen—right here in our own neighbourhood. As we say, right here in our own back yard.

As we take notice, we are reminded that once more it's all done by people. People just like you and me. Ordinary everyday people with real jobs and real families who have stepped forward and said, "How can I help," and followed what they imagined as solutions.

There are everyday miracles going on all around us, but very few are brought to our attention. We have forgotten how to recognize them. People who can imagine change and create change wherever their imagining takes them, are healing our ailing planet

Unfortunately, media dwells on the negativity and often blows it out of proportion to reinforce our fear. They say fear sells. But peace doesn't make money; it's not good for the economy, so the networks perpetuate and reinforce the negativity and the violence. People who have actually been present and who have witnessed an event, quite often comment that the incident reported by the media is not the same one that they experienced.

Is our life really based on ratings, on profits, on greed, on consumerism, on power? We are in big trouble if that is where our priorities lie. Perhaps it's time we rethink our priorities and what makes our life meaningful and joyful.

My intent is not to preach or to castigate. Paranoia runs amok, and more than enough people tell us what we should or should not be doing. You already know at your soul level what is right and what is not right. Many of us are rapidly losing hope and feeling that we can't do much anyway. Our young people are acting out in fear and abandonment and loss of hope. They feel their only recourse for drawing attention to their loneliness and desperation is violence towards themselves and towards others.

Very little can really change in how we see the world while we are being constantly bombarded with all that is bad and wrong. We feel obligated somehow to watch the news and read the newspapers. Our popular television programs are laced with violence. If it is true that we create our own reality, and this is what we are seeing and feeling day in, day out, then perhaps we are caught in our own *Groundhog Day* movie, constantly re-creating it over and over again, thereby allowing it to erode our daily lives. Even in shows designed for small children, violence is used as a form of entertainment.

After the movie *Natural Born Killers* aired, there were eighteen directly related deaths at the hands of young people who watched it and thought it would be "cool" to go out and kill a few people. The frequency of copycat killings in our schools as a way of drawing attention to angst and loneliness, anger, and fear, is escalating. How much more proof do we need before we start taking responsibility for what the media pumps into our lives everywhere we turn? Why not make a conscious effort not to watch these programs, not to read irresponsible journalism, and to question what others are forcing on us?

Our Guiding Thought

How do we involve ourselves in changing the politics of the media without getting trapped by our own anger and fear? By frustration that only adds another layer to what we believe we already perceive. *Keep it simple* should be our guiding thought.

The politics of simplicity are neither left nor right, but represent a new combination of self-reliance, community spirit, and cooperation. We must come to recognize that we are in charge, and that *one-on-one* is going to save us. The new politics are grounded in the unflinching recognition that we are being challenged to grow up and take charge of our lives, both locally and globally.

Not long ago, when John Lennon invited us to "imagine" a sweet, gracious, and peaceful world, some of us gave ourselves permission to dream. Now we must wade through layers of distractions and demands and begin to dream again. Imagine trusting the media. Imagine programs in which the news informs ethically. Imagine a world in which people actually care and are 'nice' to each other.

We have arrived at a time during which there is a world of possibility. We have the tools and the information and the ability to create the change that we long for. If we shed the quiet despair that insistently whispers that our collective lives will never make sense again, we might just find ourselves with childlike eagerness, peering expectantly into the unknown.

Our Invitation to Imagine

Can you imagine that we are at a crossroads where we clearly see ourselves as a species having evolved, grown up, and matured? We need to get out of the sandbox and reclaim what is our inherent right; our right to be happy, to be safe, and to be free. We appear to be embracing a change of thinking. Many are waking to our need for personal social wholeness and feel an urgency to respond. Something deep inside is calling. Everything we do, including making our most mundane decisions, is all part of a coherent, purposeful unfolding.

Auguste Comte (1798-1857), French founder of positivism and social reform, and inventor of the word *sociology*, put forth a "religion of humanity" that replaced the notion of God as a separate entity with the notion of humankind as a whole. Positivism may be viewed as either a philosophical system and method or as a philosophy of history. In the latter aspect, Comte's work was almost an early history of science. He attempted to reconcile science with religion. Comte believed that the human mind and its logical procedures can be known only in terms of experience, and in Comte's own view that it was at least theoretically possible that man would evolve to another stage. And how can we be sure that, although the positive method has been extended to all natural phenomena, it can be extended to human phenomena? Even if we grant this-and it is an appealing and useful assumption-does the discovery of laws regulating human phenomena put us in possession of a final science of humanity? At this point, are we not still without a science of ethics, a science that will tell us with complete positive certainty what end to pursue? In later years Comte fell deeply in love and from this love came his new emphasis on a universal religion of humanity. He sought a moral order, with the positive religion enjoining everyone "to live for others." Yet, with all the criticisms of either a conceptual or factual nature that can be levelled against Comte's position, one must not lose sight of his essential contributions in believing that man can evolve into a better human being. The same can be said of the essential contributions and influence of the media today.

Despite some of the downsides of the mass media and the Internet, they do bring to us a transparent world where injustices are increasingly difficult to hide. This transparency is bringing a new feeling of accountability and ethicality into institutional conduct.

Just imagine a new media that challenges the emotional intelligence and maturity of our species. For the first time in human history, we are acquiring a way to listen and talk with one another as members of one family on this planet. Through the immediacy of communication worldwide, we are now able to focus public awareness on injustice and violence and bring it into the light of day. When people know that the rest of the world is watching, a powerful corrective influence is brought into human relations. Martin Luther King Jr. said that to realize justice in human affairs, "injustice must be exposed, with all of the tension its exposure creates, to the light of the human conscience and the air of national opinion before it can be cured."

The global media will soon have the ability to broadcast information about virtually any place, person, issue, or event on the planet to all other places on the planet within seconds. In a communications-rich world, old forms of political repression, human rights violations, and warfare will be extremely difficult to perpetrate without an avalanche of world opinion descending on the oppressor. Is this a reflection of Comte's moral order enjoining everyone "to live for others?"

Lester Brown, president of Worldwatch Institute, stated, "The communications industry is the only instrument that has the capacity to educate on a scale that is needed and has the time available. Major networks are just now beginning to clean up their acts as the violence and sexual exploitation is no longer being passively received into our homes. We, you and I, are creating the change that is happening in our electronic as well as print media."

During my practice as a hypnotherapist, I learned how easily the mind is influenced by certain suggestions delivered in a particular manner. I've learned that through hypnotic induction techniques, thoughts, emotions, sensations, and imagery become powerful motivators, and that when applied skilfully, a major shift in belief and thought which influences a person profoundly can occur, often initiating a miraculous healing or other benefit. Unfortunately, as it is with any powerful method, this can be used for good or ill.

It is true that we are basically lazy and rely on others to tell us how we should think, feel, and act. We are fearful of trusting our deep intuition. There are those in our modern world who take advantage of this, so that we are bombarded everyday with deliberate and manipulative stimulation through television, radio, newspapers, magazines, and now the worldwide web, by people who know what they are doing, people who often appeal to the lowest common denominator in humanity.

We live in a culture that overstimulates us on many levels, to the point where it becomes more difficult for us to know who we really are, what we really want, and how we really think. Everywhere we look, we see images of the "ideal" body, the "ideal" lifestyle, relationship, job, etc. In order to "fit in," and be an accepted member of the so-called *normal* community, we are greatly pressured to conform in some fashion. We're pressured into making the "right" amount of money so that we can purchase a larger house, a new car, fashionable clothing—things that will ensure that we are respected, admired and accepted, all of which leads to happiness. Or so we are to believe.

In 1973, I sold my television set. As a single mom with five small children all under the age of ten, that seemed insane. But I felt guilty using television as a handy babysitter. To take its place, we all enrolled in music and dance lessons, and I had the children take out individual library cards. Long forgotten board games of Christmases past became fun again, and so did quiet time as each of us found our own space in which to be creative. There was even time to imagine.

For a while, I stopped reading national newspapers, tuned in to public broadcasting, and kept abreast of local politics in my own community. The children and I would sit around in the evening listening to stories that were actually more visual than watching television. We spent time in dialogue, and the children were content in just being quiet. This helped to lift the veil that had prevented me from really seeing humanity and the world in an enlightened, expansive, and positive way.

But so many conversations on the playground were geared to what had been on the tube the night before, the children felt out of the loop with their peers. This was creating a gap, so I acquiesced to letting them watch television at their friends' on certain days or evenings, depending on the programming. They did not push us to buy a new TV because they liked the family closeness and interaction that was going on in their own home.

Years later, a well intentioned friend gifted us with a large new television set, and I caved. I noticed that little had changed in the negative reporting techniques, but shock effect and rumour mongering were now more prevalent. This time I saw the programming more clearly.

Eliminating "media madness" has sharpened my awareness. I am less inclined to be swayed by consensus opinion. My research has unfortunately confirmed the hypothesis that if you spend your days on the Net or watch hours of television daily, you are generally not drawn or motivated to reading books or to taking part in dialogue that requires thinking "outside the box;" you have allowed your mind to "dumb-down." The old adage, "if you don't use it, you lose it" applies here. The brain is like a muscle and requires exercise. It needs to get out of the groove you got yourself stuck in.

The Net Turns Sour

Steve Maich, (*Maclain's Magazine*, October 2006), wrote an article "The Internet Sucks (Where did we go wrong?)." He writes that the idealist who conceived and pioneered the Web had predicted a kind of enlightened utopia built on mutual understanding, a world in which knowledge is limited only by one's curiosity.

Maich states that: "Instead, we have constructed a virtual Wild West, where the masses indulge their darkest vices, pirates of all kinds troll for victims, and the rest of us have come to accept that cyberspace isn't the kind of place we'd want to raise our kids. The great multinational exchange of ideas and goodwill has devolved into a food fight, and the virtual marketplace is a great place to get robbed. The answers to the great questions of our world may be out there somewhere, but finding them will require you to first wade through an ocean of misinformation, trivia and sludge." Steve Maich writes: "Conspiracy theories, conjecture and outright fabrications masquerade as fact on the Internet, and often, nobody seems to notice the difference. The problem is rooted equally in the nature of humans and the nature of cyberspace. The designers of the Internet put their deepest faith in the wisdom of the masses to establish truth and value by consensus. The real problem is that, with the spreading influence of the Internet, we are trading in authoritative and accurate for cheap and convenient." Maich goes on to say, "And so, in an era in which we're supposed to have universal access to more information from more varied sources around the world, there are fewer and fewer reporters on the ground digging up original information. And the companies in the business of providing credible, original reporting are finding it more and more difficult to survive." [7]

George Will, *Newsweek*'s revered columnist, wrote a few years back. "It is no exaggeration to conclude that the Internet has achieved, and continues to achieve, the most participatory marketplace of mass speech that this country—and indeed the world has yet seen."

Sounds spectacular, but what's the great value of a participatory marketplace of mass speech if so few have anything to say that's worth buying. There are certainly some interesting and insightful blogs on a wide range of topics. But in general, the more substantive the subject matter, the less reliable the commentary is. The vast majority of political blogs are deeply ideological and partisan, and as such, they attract a core of like-minded contributors whose writings tend to devolve into vitriolic screeds or sophomoric insults.

In a 2001 paper, Cass Sunstein, a professor at the University of Chicago Law School, described the "echo chamber" effect of blogs and message boards. Rather than fostering debate, moderation, and common understanding, he argues that these sites have contributed to the polarization of our political culture. "People gravitate toward sites that reflect their established point of view, and once comfortably ensconced in their political echo chamber, the participants take turns preaching to the assembled choir, reinforcing each other's ideas and biases, and denouncing any one who might disagree."

Rather than promoting open discussion and greater understanding, the Net has fed the cynical perception that every form of traditional authority is based on lies and corruption. The much-hyped free market of ideas is a world in which the loudest and the most outrageous assertion dominates the discussion. Everybody believes they are being oppressed by those opposed to them. The truth is what you already think it is, and nobody is going to change your mind and nobody can be trusted.

Grooving Your Brain

Repetitive statements, thoughts, and imagery have a profound impact on the mind. If we are exposed often enough and long enough to the same kinds of stimulus, over and over again, it will wear a literal groove in the brain; a particular neuronal pathway becomes deeply etched, and one's thoughts become confined to their own familiar pathways and demonstrate certain responses called "habits." Habits include recurring thoughts as well as recurring behaviour.   Just as a path is worn down as our feet walk across a pristine field, the same way do our predominate thoughts carve out a ravine in our brain by which our behaviour becomes entrenched; we move from thought to behaviour along this pathway that leads us again and again to the same reaction. This locks us into patterns that, as we age, become more and more difficult to change.

In the external world, when we walk the same old path again and again, we see the same old scenery again and again, and eventually, it becomes so familiar to us that we no longer see it. So it is within; the more entrenched in our thinking we become by dialoguing with those who agree with us, the more intense our conviction that we see the world truly, when in reality, we have ceased to see at all.

Remember the runaway coach in a previous chapter, and how it lulled the owner into a deep sleep? By interactions like those I've just described, we allow this to happen to ourselves.

Our Thoughts and Beliefs—Where Did They Come From?

Have you ever wondered how all those thoughts got inside your head in the first place? Would you find it hard to believe that someone else put them there? When we were tiny babies, we didn't "think" about anything. This was before we acquired language and the ability to understand and use it. We simply acted on impulse in the moment. Hungry? Cry. Hurt? Cry some more. Gotta go? Pee. Want that shiny thing? Reach for it. Delighted? Laugh out loud. Tired? Sleep. Don't like it? Scream. There were no thoughts, and we had no beliefs that we were cognisant of. There was no right or wrong, no "shoulds" or "should nots." But eventually we were exposed to language, beliefs, and behavioural patterns, and they conditioned us. So all those words that you hear in your head came from somebody else; you just took them all on as your own.

No Thought

The vast majority of us have yet to experience the mind without thought. Some of us call that 'state' of mind "meditation" or "quieting the mind." I truly believe that it is the realm of "no-thought" that brings us home to our true and natural state of being. But we certainly have a long way to go, for most of us spend our days with our "monkey brains" running and hoping around everywhere, and those of us who do "zone out," are usually in a state of mindlessness. So where am I going with all of this?

The mind is powerful. Scientific evidence proves that the thinking and imagery that one is exposed to and dwells on, influences the health of both mind and body, and how he or she perceives the world.

Replacing the Old with the New

We believe that it's a modern notion that you are not your body but I doubt there's a single variation on this idea that isn't at least several thousand years old. It's true, you *are* far more than a body; the body eventually peters out, but your spirit/soul leaves a lasting imprint and moves on to another existence. This is fodder for another book at another time. However, you do have a body, and it is easily influenced by your circumstances, thoughts, beliefs, and what you feed it physically, emotionally, and intellectually.

Though this has been said many times before, the key to our liberation is often in being exposed to an important revelation over and over again. This is the way we tread new neuronal pathways through the landscape of our brains. In so doing, liberating revelation and new thoughts replace, sooner than later, the obsolete thinking that binds us to the past and imprisons us in the land of limitation into which we've locked ourselves.

What I learned all those years ago as a practising hypnotherapist makes all the sense in the world now, and it has changed my life in profound and wondrous ways. Working, listening, and hearing with an open non-judgemental mind to people's thoughts and beliefs has given me an incredible gift that enables me to peel back some of my own very deeply embedded blinders.

The following was written by Willis Harmon, former president of the Institute for Noetic Sciences which was founded by Edgar Mitchell, the astronaut who walked on the moon in 1971. Harmon was the author of *Global Mind Change and Higher Creativity: Liberating the Unconscious for Breakthrough Insights.* He wrote "Reprogramming the unconscious beliefs that block fuller awareness of our creative/intuitive capabilities depends upon a key characteristic of the unconscious mind, namely, that it responds to what is vividly imagined essentially as though it were a real experience." [8]

What Willis Harmon is telling us is that to change the way we see and understand life around us, we need to vividly imagine and feel and nurture new beliefs. Imagine the feelings and beliefs you create within yourself when you watch violence on television or at the movies. Imagine what happens to your neuronal pathways when you are bombarded with repetitive advertising. Your brain and central nervous system do not know the difference between what they see on the screen and what they see in real life; they respond as though everything is true. Eventually you have fed yourself a series of beliefs that become real to you.

Ever notice how your body becomes tense during a suspenseful scene in a high action movie? This is a perfect example of this effect. It doesn't make a bit of difference that logic tells you that it's only a movie—your brain and central nervous system are viewing it and recording it as an actual event.

Harmon tells us how to replace old, undesirable beliefs.

"Because the unconscious beliefs have been re-experienced or re-affirmed repeatedly over a long period of time, the substitute beliefs and/or images must also be presented repetitiously over a period of time, preferably in a state of deep relaxation when the portals of the unconscious are most open." Harmon goes on to say that in a peaceful, relaxed state, we can open our minds to change, that we can release our intuition and creativity and, as a result, go ahead to live our lives with clearer intent. When you act spontaneously without previous thought, you experience one of the most natural, miraculous, clearest, and most liberated states of being.

There are many practical applications of this principle—the principle being that what we affirm and program into the unconscious belief system, we tend in subtle ways to bring about. When we establish and affirm an intention or goal—imagining that it is already so—the unconscious mind is programmed to achieve that goal. To achieve it, it will use ways which the conscious part of the mind does not plan or understand.

Athletic coaches, for instance, train athletes to image championship performance. Some doctors and healers train cancer patients to heal themselves by imagining the immune system ridding the body of cancer cells. Business executives mentally affirm that desired goals are already achieved. It's said that when Jim Thorpe, the great American Indian athlete, was aboard a ship on his way across the ocean with the American Olympic team, his coach asked why he was sitting on deck rather than actively training. Thorpe answered that he was seeing himself win the decathlon, and he did go on to win it.

This has long been a core idea in the esoteric inner-core of the Christian tradition. The basic principal is found in Mark 11:24. "Whatever you ask in prayer, believe that you receive it and you will." The prayer I am speaking of being a process of thoughts and projections in a mindful state.

In practice, the process of changing the unconsciously held beliefs may not seem as simple as just represented. As earlier noted, we tend to resist new information or experiences that threaten the unconscious belief system. A hypnotized person will vociferously deny evidence that conflicts with his hypnotically induced perceptions. He or she will go to all lengths to explain why behaviour directed by a post-hypnotic suggestion is really perfectly reasonable behaviour. By this, I mean behaviour in response to a suggestion from the hypnotist, which the subject does not remember, cued by a signal of which the subject is unaware. The phenomenon of denial is familiar in psychotherapy; the client will actually fail to see what is apparent to any onlooker, because to see it would be too threatening.

Psychologist Abraham Maslow wrote eloquently about this in *Toward a Psychology of Being Entitled*. In his chapter, "On the Need to Know and the Fear of Knowing," Maslow observed that we are all ambivalent when it comes to knowing ourselves. We may consciously intend to use affirmations to reprogram the unconscious, and then, because of inner resistance, we "forget" to carry out the exercises. We want to know where we are deceiving ourselves, but at the same time, we will go to great lengths to avoid finding out. We have been thoroughly taught in Western culture not to trust ourselves, not to trust that ultimately we DO know what we most deeply desire, and how to resolve our inner conflicts. We have been taught that beneath the thin veneer of the socialized conscious mind lurk who-knows-what animal urges, repressed hostilities, and other evils. We have been taught not to risk exploring the unconscious mind, at least, not without a psychiatrist seated alongside in case we get into trouble.

And so we are reluctant to uncover the fearsome and unsavoury about ourselves. But as Maslow points out, "We find another kind of resistance, a denying of our best side, of our talents, of our finest impulse, of our highest potentialities, of our creativeness. It is precisely the god-like in ourselves that we are ambivalent about, fascinated by and fearful of, motivated to and defensive against."

Go Ahead and Do It

Turn off the noise. Choose instead to expose your mind to those external effects that tend to inspire rather than appall. View educational and enlightening programs, movies, and plays. Listen to beautiful and uplifting music through recordings or concerts. Read inspirational literature and appreciate fine art. Hang out with your friends and talk about the finer, more interesting, more enjoyable things in life rather than gossiping about others and fear mongering. Focus more on what's right in the world rather than on what's wrong in it. Spend more time with nature, with loved ones, with babies, with animals or whoever gives you joy. Walk more and try to catch the sunrises as well as the wonderful sunsets we're so often blessed with. Take time to be aware of your breathing and "smell the roses" as much as you can. Give yourself these gifts; they are priceless. And just watch and see how much more enjoyable the world—and you—will become!

So turn the television off and go and find yourself. Don't worry about the virtual wild West of the Internet. America was once the "Wild West," and so was Australia, but eventually, because the human spirit is basically good, we tame ourselves. We just need to be given a little shake to wake up from our complacency.

Earlier, I mentioned that Edgar Mitchell walked on the moon in 1971. During his return flight, Dr. Mitchell had a life changing experience, an epiphany. To quote him directly, "I experienced an ecstasy of unity. I not only saw the connectedness, I felt it and experienced it sentiently. The restraints and boundaries of flesh and bone fell away."

Many others have described the same experience. This connectiveness, this experience of oneness, this awareness that we are not our bodies and that we are all one, is the deepest form of enlightenment. After returning to Earth, Dr. Mitchell retired from NASA and founded the Institute of Noetic Sciences, an organization that does research into the nature of consciousness.

We ask, "What *is* consciousness?" As we try to *de*fine it, we *con*fine it. It's like trying to describe a thought, a feeling, or what music tastes like.

Chapter 7

Understanding Consciousness and Responsibility: The Ability to Respond

"All things whatsoever ye would that men should do to you, do ye even so to them."
—Mathew 7:12

Globally, people are seeking to understand what we are doing here in the first place and why we as a species continue to try to kill each other. Why are we trying to self-destruct and destroy the world along with us. Global despair is forcing us to look at the "elephant in the living room"—several elephants, in fact: terrorism, ethnic cleansing, poverty, child abuse, greed, and global pollution. I hoped we would never see the elephant called terrorism. In all honesty, along with most of you, I feel rather impotent in dealing with this very real and present danger. Until we have some understanding of how we hold them in our minds and how their minds embrace these acts and the circumstances that have brought them to this place, we will not be able to move forward in our rightful claim to peace and freedom from this terrible menace.

Plundering, pilfering, poverty, polluting, and ethnic cleansing are old movies that are no longer acceptable in our twenty-first century consciousness—or so we say, although this very scenario continues to play itself out even in our time.

We in our Western world tend to draw back, to not get involved; even so, as terrorism encroaches on our way of life, we will respond. But until it affects us in our pocketbooks and/or personal comforts, most of us won't feel pressed to enter the fray.

Most of the land in our world has been claimed, reclaimed, divided, conquered, pilfered, and plundered over and over again, most times not in fair and just ways. We act out the scarcity principle under whose guise we try to gain more—just in case there is not enough. Might becomes right. We use violence and power for what we think we need, or because we feel that we're superior or special, and we see others as less valuable than we. We seem to think that people are commodities and easily replaceable, even when they are the same color, and dress and speak as we do. We want what they have—just in case there's not enough to fill our ever-demanding need for more comfort and more things.

In addition to our insatiable acquisitiveness, we presume to know what others should believe and how they should behave, and we attempt to impose our way of life upon them—believing that our way is the only way.

War of the Gods

We buy into the belief that "my god is bigger than your god." People fight over matters of belief. It matters not one whit whether it's so-called Christians fighting Christians or Christians fighting other religions, or whether Muslims are fighting Muslims. Whatever religion one wants to claim as his or her own, it's the same. We tend to group over issues or to soldier gather, and the more numbers we have, the more we're convinced that we're right.

This warring, especially in established religions, reflects the idea that a god chooses certain groups of people to personally represent him, (usually the god is male.) This god has many human personality traits and is a very needy, warring, and jealous god. These "special" chosen people fight for him, suffer for him, and live for him, in order to appease and please him so they can remain on his good side.

Interestingly, this same god almost always has no love for the female species that he created. He acts as if he is fearful of them and must keep them at bay because of their enticing, magic powers. Intellectual discourse or dialogue or a smidgen of common sense can't seem to find a niche in regard to this and many other issues within these religions.

At this present time, a small group of self-imposed Islamic spiritual leaders are repeating what a group of Christians did in another time and place. As I write this my mind keeps on revisiting the movie *The Mission*. And this small group of extremists are tightening the noose of fear around the Western world's neck, attempting to hold us hostage. They wish to intimidate or kill everyone who is not part of their belief system, and they have little concern for the innocents who die in the process.

We don't know how to respond to this. We do not wish to offend. Our beliefs clash with theirs, but we fear the repercussions of that disagreement. We don't have a clear definition of what they want from us—other than seeing us annihilated. They don't want our land. They don't want our resources.

They don't want our women or children. And they especially do not want our way of life. These so-called Islamic leaders are rewriting the doctrines of a once great religion that brought the world some of its finest minds and teachers. Now they are teaching self-serving fear and violence.

Abbot Mingzing, a teacher of Islam and the Abrahamic tradition stated:

> We firmly believe in the truism that all faiths are the paths leading towards the Ultimate Reality, just as the spokes of the wheel converge to its axis. When the people are too immersed in the dogmas and rituals of their chosen religion, it appears to them to be the only one worth following and they defend their own particular faith. However, when they have acquired enough wisdom, charity and discernment, they too are bound to perceive that the road to heaven is nobody's monopoly and that the Divine laws apply equally to all. It is the dogmas, ritual and the mode of worship that divide the faiths and not the basic essence of their beliefs. But I am not in favour of conversion from one faith to another; neither do I believe in the fusion of all religions into one. The Ultimate Truth is one, but it has an infinite number of aspects and what is more beautiful than that each faith should reflect only one facet of the Divine, all of them together creating a shining gem of beauty. Would the world be more if all the flowers on Earth had been blended into one uniform color or all mountains razed to make the globe monotonously flat? Each religion offers something glorious, peculiarly its own, to point out the road to the Ultimate Reality. What man or group of men would be able to prescribe a single form of religion that would satisfy all and everybody? That would be an attempt to give a finite concept of the Infinite and of course, it would fail.

When ancient Islamic teachings are brought to the attention of these modern present-day fundamentalist "spiritual leaders," and when their teachings are even *questioned*, they cry *Infidel!* and order a jihad or death threat to anyone who dares think differently. There is no space or opening for discourse or discussion.

History is testimony to the great impulses brought to humanity by the great educators—the prophets. And Jesus revealed the *spirit behind the forms* of the laws of Moses! He introduced the concept of God = Love. Muhammad, like all the prophets, upheld the same, one foundation. We can see the same purpose behind all the prophets of God. They were the sources of spiritual empowerment, elevation, and order to the communities to which they were sent. The various scriptures or holy books contained the primary divine revelations that of necessity were adapted to the style and expression of a given people at a given historical period. As Junayd (d.298) the Sufi Imam of the World in his time wrote, "Water takes on the color of its container."

Several specific world faiths have emerged from the Abrahamic "tree." For Westerners, this is the most recognizable religious inheritance. But I am not excluding from true faiths the venerable religions of the Orient such as Buddhism, Hinduism, Zoroastrianism, or even the illustrious so-called "pagan" wisdom of the Greeks, Egyptians, Sumerians and others.

Indeed, all the great religions of antiquity can be appreciated through the divine conception. Christianity and Islam represent the heritage of the primordial tradition according to specific historical development. The European Muslim writer Michel Valsan points out:

> The Islamic doctrine is formal on the point that all the Divine Messengers have brought essentially the same message and that all the traditions are in essence one. Islam, as the last of the revealed religions in the Abrahamic stream has an intimate relationship with the other two and axiomatically expresses the Divine Conception of Religion. A religion based principally on knowledge compared to its predecessor Christianity based on love. Here is a vital example of unfolding revelation. Out of the Abrahamic "tree," the Torah emphasized the Divine Law preparing the way for the Gospels that emphasized the element of Divine Love. Islam, while acknowledging the two former revelations, emphasised Divine Knowledge. Abdul Latif of Sind proclaimed: "Love and Intellect are the two wings of the bird."

This is the beauty and truth of Islam. But this is not the Islam that the majority of the Western world understands. We are mostly aware of a small group of thugs who hold us all hostage. Intellectual sharing and common sense avail nothing with them. We are afraid of offending them, so we give them ground and have encouraged the movement to grow and to gain strength. Legitimate world organizations and recognized government bodies keep feeding them with funds and support. Extremist groups around the world have now turned to the Internet as a powerful recruiting tool. Many who feel estranged or downtrodden will believe that this is the answer to their angst. This empowers such persons and gives them a reason to be.

Patrons of Peace

So how do we deal with this powerful movement? "Kicking ass" does not seem to be the answer, nor will this method *ever* work, because it only strengthens their resolve. Dangerous stuff we are dealing with. We feel that our world is regressing and being held in a time warp.

James Twyman in his book, *Portrait of the Master*, tells a story of Saint Francis of Assisi, the patron saint of animals, of the environment, and of peace. Almost eight hundred years ago, Francis journeyed to Egypt to meet with the sultan. He travelled with the crusaders, not to fight the Muslins, or even to preach to them, but to persuade them and the Christians to make peace and live together in harmony. Saint Francis was captured, thrown into prison, and then granted an extraordinary meeting with the sultan. The conversation they exchanged focused on compassion and seeing only good in each other. In this story Francis says, "I have discovered how simple the truth is." And he tells us that the sultan replies, "… You have built a bridge between two great oceans, my heart and my mind."[9]

But those Islamic fundamentalists who are now bringing terror upon the world are not like this honorable sultan. How do we "do nice" with leaders and groups who are closed to any rational thinking? How do we come to know and understand what it will take to heal this ongoing wound? The answer is education, education, education. The new generation of Islamic and Christian children must be given the choice of seeing with new eyes. While I was writing this little book, I was privileged to be on a mailing list of a young Canadian major serving in Afghanistan. His weekly journal opened my eyes to the reality that the world needs to make a responsible effort in being there. These few words helped me understand the servitude under which the average Afghan lives.

> The town looked like it could have been pulled out of time a thousand years ago. Mud/straw buildings with walls two feet thick. Homes were an outer wall with one entrance, a door of wood or metal. Inside is a courtyard with a well and outdoor cooking oven. Typically, rooms were bubbled off the interior of the outer walls. A typical home has two rooms, a common area and a sleeping area, with the whole complex about 10 metres X 10 metres. No electricity, running water or sewage system. There are no spaces between homes; they share adjoining walls, so the streets are long corridors with doors along them, no windows anywhere except inside the compounds in the rooms to provide light. I found the closed and oppressive nature of this town very much reflected the constraints of the society, or perhaps it's the other way round. Does the social structure demand the physical barriers to hold it together? Either way, we made a few new openings in the buildings of this town; hopefully it will help with the social structure.

The young major commented that many of the suicide bombers were farmers forced to work the poppy fields, people who had no awareness of a future or of another choice of life. Many are high on opium and have been indoctrinated by the war lords to kill for Allah.

Somewhere, I have read that if there is a crack in the darkness, that little bit of light will eventually light up the whole room.

The comment, "we made a few new openings in the buildings of this town; hopefully it will help with the social structure," struck a strong cord within me. By assisting with reconstruction and by spending social time with these people our young men and women are hoping to bring in a ray of light that will, over time, bring in "enlightenment."

Our own young people today also need a ray of light, a hope for a better tomorrow. Many express their impotence through violence and isolation. Some search for their own tribe through their body art and unusual dress. Some numb their feelings of fear and loneliness through the vast menu of very accessible drugs, alcohol and life threatening addictions, gambling, shopping, sex, or violence. This has become the Russian roulette of the twenty-first century. Some join cults, religions, and organizations that offer *specialness*. Some are quick to make their mark in the pursuit of great wealth without the attachment of consequences. Work addiction is a great motivator for some; by it, they acquire more land, larger houses, the latest tech toys, vehicles, clothes, name brands, and the accumulation of luxuries in today's marketplace that give external signs of control. We are selling our souls in the pursuit of the mantra that *there is never enough*.

Some choose, through a passion for excellence, to made great breakthroughs in technology, science, and medicine. In the arts, many make intellectual and artistic achievements that force others to think outside the box.

Despite the plethora of choices, others are choosing creative simplicity. Some are opting out of the predominant social milieu to homestead, return to the land, or seek out alternative lifestyles. They choose not to buy into the chaos of Life 101.

Fortunately many of those who opt out choose to become their brother's keeper. They choose to give their lives to those who are trapped by their innocence and circumstances. They are involved in creating safe havens for young girls and boys sold into the sex trade, rescuing children from enslavement and horrible living conditions both in our Western world and in third world countries. They are helping to dig wells, build schools, hospitals, road and bridges. They use their teaching skills and knowledge of the trades generously. They practice medicine "without borders" and without financial compensation. They give of themselves day in and day out without the trappings and comforts into which they were born.

It does not matter what method we use, what reason we have, or in what way we choose to help others. The way each of us deals with the present world simply reflects our feelings about the way things are. There is no place we can go to escape from the world around us. We are now a global community and there is a growing discomfort, as injustice is repeatedly made real in our daily lives.

People of every age and cultural background want to belong to some form of community, even if it is to be part of those who chose *not to belong*, not to conform. We seek out companionship with those of like mind, or we seek out solitude and peace in nature. Some of us just want some quiet amid the chaos of our busy daily-ness, while others are afraid to stop the noise and action, too fearful of looking at our reality, our loneliness. Some are becoming inured to the *dis*-ease around us, but most of us, as we watch the daily re-creation of violence and fear played out on our doorstep, are uneasy with our impotence

Amongst us, there are small armies of people young and old who are choosing to put their livelihood and life at risk to become stewards of our environment, of the planet we cohabit. There are those who are choosing to be "the watchers"who speak out about man's inhumanity to man. Young and old are choosing to take an active role in their communities and neighbourhoods; they are choosing to care for each other. Many choose to question the politics of the day and to actively seek change. They choose to recognize that politics and change can only come from the grass roots up. They choose to see that the answer is "one person at a time."

Daring to Question

Many of us question the teachings of some of our churches and other religious organizations that foster fear, bigotry, bias and/or injustice. What is true of some churches is also true of politics and corporate life. There are many, in reality a growing number of concerned citizens, forming organizations, making our politicians aware that they are not representing our best interests. They and we tend to forget that we gave these politicians their jobs in the first place. Some of us are actually doing something about it, no longer just verbally complaining, but being proactive in bringing political representation to task. Many in the corporate world are beginning to take action as stewards of our planet and are finding that by greening and bringing integrity into corporate practices, their companies have become more fiscally responsible.

Time appears to be quickening for many of us. Is it because we are aging and have not yet resolved our souls' journeys and yet are closer to dropping our bodies? Or is it because the world that we have created is tired and ready to shrug us off and host those with more awareness that she, Mother Earth, is a living and breathing being, not to be repeatedly raped and defiled.

Perhaps in this dream we all share, it is time we showed recognition for her beauty and her incredible generosity of spirit. The time has come to recognize how forgiving she is as she constantly replenishes what we have taken despite our lack of putting into place a returning cycle.

Our Warming Earth

Climate change is arguably among the most serious issues facing the planet. No part of Earth is safe from global warming, and North America is particularly vulnerable. Will our elected leaders act on the scientific evidence, or will they bow to the lobbyists representing the most polluting corporations in order to gain their financial support or to fill the coffers of their friends who own these industries?

What are our governments and corporations doing right here, right now about these issues? Some innovative business leaders in traditional and new industries are actually reducing emissions while expanding their profitability and opportunities and discovering bottom-line gain in environmental stewardship. China is giving lip service to being a good steward because of the upcoming games in Beijing, but her coal emissions in 2006 created havoc on Canada's pristine west coast, destroying grandfather trees that were hundreds of years old. The storms uprooted old growth and majestic trees in world famous Stanley Park, their beauty never to be experienced again in our lifetime. But we are all responsible as we stay stuck in our mindless state and sit in our impotency.

The big rich countries and the big rich companies roam freely in the international trading system. The rules of the game are set up by the global institutions with their predatory sensitivities to the needs of those countries and companies, and insensitivities to the needs of humanity and Earth herself. Poor countries, the least-developed countries where most of the world's people live, are weakened by their poverty, and yet they still must play in the field of the international trading system. Such are the asymmetries of wealth and power that plague this planet. As Gandhi said, "We have enough for everyone's need, but not for everyone's greed." What can we do? What must be done?

Signs that Give Hope

Something very promising emerged at a conference in May 2002 in Nairobi—an initiative that mobilizes lawyers and economists to offer their expertise on trade, free on request, to the smallest and poorest countries. It's called International Lawyers and Economists against Poverty. Lawyers and economists—neither profession, known for its humanitarian stance—have come together for the greater good. This in itself is a remarkable change in the consciousness of mankind, and helps us remember that all that is done is done by and with people. Presently, many governments are meeting globally and many are passing new legislation that includes environmental practises for new building codes, energy usage, agricultural practices, water and air protection. Voices are being heard and changes are being made.

One of the powerful facts about the present-day environmental movement is that much of the best momentum for change is coming from within the industry rather than from governments or the non-governmental organizations that have spent decades raising awareness. This is a phenomenon so counterintuitive that it has taken even the captains of industry by surprise. It seems unusual now to have industry and environmentalists working together, but it is the way of the future. Now the need is greater then ever to bring integrity and fiscal responsibility to financial institutions and to our government so that we will not have a repeat of Enron or a continuance of the present vast government waste.

It is *we* who are making these gains, *we* individuals, and *we* small groups who know that the time is ripe and that there is an urgency for change at a spiritual level within these institutions. There is no other way.

Duane Elgin in his book *Promises Ahead* writes:

> We are seeing trends that have the power to fuel an evolutionary bounce. One is the power of perception and the emergence of a perceptual paradigm that allows us to see the universe as alive rather than dead. Another is the power of choice and our ability to shift voluntarily toward a simpler way of life. A third is the power of communication and the opportunity to use the Internet and the mass media to support a quantum increase in conversation about our common future. The fourth trend that has the capacity to transform a crash into a bounce— the power of love. By this I mean not romantic love, but a mature and soulful compassion that looks beneath surface differences and sees our common connection with the community of life.[10]

"Love," said Teilhard de Chardin, "is the fundamental impulse of Life—the one natural medium in which the rising course of evolution can proceed." Without love, he said, "there is truly nothing ahead of us except the forbidding prospect of standardization and enslavement—the doom of ants and termites."

The Golden Rule

We have reached the point where the Golden Rule is becoming essential to humanity's survival. This ancient ethic, which is found in all of the worlds' spiritual traditions, advises that the way to know how to treat others is to know how we want to be treated.

"As you wish that men would do to you, do so to them," from Luke 6:31 is Christianity's expression of the Golden Rule.

"No one of you is a believer until he desires for his brother that which he desires for himself," said Sunan. The golden rule according to Islam.

In the teachings of the Buddha (Udanavarga) the Golden Rule expresses itself in this way, "Hurt not others in ways that you yourself would find hurtful."

"Do naught unto others that which would cause you pain of done to you." Hinduism (Mahabharata 5:1517)

"Do not unto others what you would not have them do unto you." Confucianism (Analetcts 15:23)

Ancient teachings are simply asking us to be *nice*, to be *delicate* with each other. This is something that has been asked of us of for thousands of years from all religious and spiritual teachers. So how can we live on this planet and not buy into the mass consciousness of fear and the belief that there is not enough, and to recognize that we are all equal, that by being *nice* to each other we may create the change that we long for?

Remember that at the beginning of this book I mentioned that this was your/my world. That you really don't need to do anything or change anything except how you feel about yourself. When you feel good enough about your self, when you are aware that there is nothing wrong with you, then you begin to create change, and you begin to bring your brother along because it just feels right to do so. Being enlightened or mindful simply means to share who you are and what you know.

Being Self-aware

As Teilhard de Chardin says: "The being that is the object of his own reflection, in consequence of that very doubling back upon himself, becomes in a flash able to raise himself into a new sphere."

Nicely put. We are all reflections of each other simply in different space suits with different circumstances, all from the same source with the same agenda and purpose. Some of us just more conscious than others. That does not make the more conscious ones better, just more aware or more enlightened. Time to pass on some of that light to others.

Duane Elgin in his book, *Promises Ahead,* also speaks about the importance of the awakening of own species, Homo sapiens. Humans are supposed to have wisdom, but we are also supposed to be doubly wise. Animals know, but we humans "know that we know."

In *The Phenomenon of Man*, Teilhard de Chardin says that when the first living creature consciously "perceived itself in its own mirror, the whole world took a pace forward." The capacity we have as individuals and as a species when we self-observe, when we begin an examined life, is not trivial—it has the potential to create great change; an explosively powerful capacity that has given a supercharged boost to the evolutionary process.

When you, I, we—as a group, a nation, or better still, as an entire species—"know that we know," when we actually self-observe, we can begin to take responsibility for our actions. For the first time in our history, humanity is beginning to awaken to the fact of what it means to "know that we know." When the species consciously recognizes itself as a single community with responsibility to the rest of life, both present and future, we will cross the threshold to a new level of maturity, and a new culture and consciousness will begin to grow in the world.

Our species has been stuck in our sandbox far too long, and it's time to be nudged out of our complacency and grow into healthy adolescents. It is time to break out of our comfort zone and begin to explore our individuality, ready to say no to our parents (the system), to the social structure in which we find ourselves—and which we created—and to reexamine our spiritual nature. Many are saying that it is time for change. Time for a revolution from within us. Time to look through new eyes. Time to explore the meaning of being responsible and what it is to be conscious.

Waiting for the Cavalry

So why are we not doing something and taking personal action towards change? I think that everyone who has considered these matters has at the back of her mind—the same as I have at the back of mine—*a faith in miracles that grades seamlessly into excuses for inaction.* We place a lot of hope in unproven technologies and that "they"—the unidentifiable, omnipotent scientists—won't let the collapse of the biosphere happen. Our governments will not allow terrorism to rule our lives and permit us to be imprisoned in our own fear.

We don't want the solution to affect our pocket book, and we definitely do want someone else to do it for us. There was a time when we were willing to lie on the road to protect some trees or owls, and those authorities who sat on high responded and created parks and sanctuaries. Now we sit on our broadening backsides and moan about the fact that everyone else is moaning about the fact and that no one is doing anything.

George Monbiot is a journalist, environmental activist, and a visiting professor at Oxford Brookes University. He has won the UN Global 500 award for outstanding environmental achievement. In his new book *Heat: How to Stop the Planet from Burning*, writes:

This is partly, I think, because of the sustained global economic growth between then and now. We are simply too comfortable, and we have too much to lose. It is partly also because, accompanying this growth (indeed to some extent driving it) has been a surge in indebtedness, especially among the young, who used to be on the front line. Debt induces a bright panic, which ensures that those burdened with it can seldom see beyond the next few weeks." [11]

It is interesting that all the *stuff* we worked so hard to accumulate, all the things we thought we needed to make us happy and successful, is the very *stuff* that is holding us back. This *stuff* keeps us driving our coach out of control, the horses running with blinders on, and we keep rushing toward being consumed in a toxic and false world of our own making.

The Internet is a wondrous and useful tool, but it has created a false sense that something is being done. It has allowed us to believe that we can change the world without leaving our chairs as we blog, email, interact, and debate with others "out there." Yes, we are being heard, and yes, a movement is growing, but all of this is of value only if it inspires action. But do we ask what kind of action? Do we ponder what we are supposed to be doing to create the change we want?

Remember again, how, at the beginning of this little book, I said that all you have to do is change how you feel about yourself?

Taking the Leap

Examine your life with the express purpose of changing how you feel about you, and you will take an imaginative leap. Seldom has anyone demanded of you such a leap as you will take. It will be a leap for the campaign against climate change, against world hunger and poverty, and against all that plagues us.

But this campaign is an odd one. Unlike the public protests which have preceded it, it is a campaign not for abundance but for simplicity. It is a campaign not for more freedom from without, but a freedom from within. Strangest of all, it is a campaign against our old selves. It is a campaign for *mindfulness*.

If we remain inactive because we don't want to leave our comfort zone, because we have mortgaged ourselves to the hilt, and our credit cards are maxed out, whose problem *is* this?

Think of the word *responsible*. It means simply "to be able to respond." It is an absolute fact that before I can respond to others and my world, I must respond to myself. If I can respond to self, hopefully a *conscious* self, then that is all that need be said. So what does a conscious self entail, and once again what is the meaning of consciousness? And how can I *leap* into it?

Consciousness from Matter, or Matter from Consciousness?

Consciousness may be defined as awareness—experientially, personally, as an awareness that *you* exist, and that you are aware of the environment in which you exist. Consciousness enables you to react to changes in yourself and/or in your environment.

Though the topic of consciousness has been with us for centuries, it is difficult to develop a systematic and holistic theory of its organization and structure. Let's see if we can develop such a theory.

I'm going to undertake this task in a unique and entirely original manner, emphasizing the relevance of an interdisciplinary approach that focuses on science as well as on the humanities.

Andrew Lohrey of the University of Tasmania, working from a new nonrationalist, nonmaterialist framework, breaks with the habits of reasoned materialism that sustain objective approaches to consciousness. He does this to avoid the typical question of how consciousness arises from matter. In a startling reversal, he instead inquires about how *matter* arises from *consciousness*. He determines that consciousness, like quantum mechanics, cannot be analyzed and treated by reductionistic or mechanical means; it needs an approach compatible with *its inclusive and circular character*.

Lohrey, in his *The Meaning of Consciousness,* draws on a range of thinkers to emphasize the interconnections of spirituality, psychology, and physics. His work is groundbreaking and puts a whole new understanding to the idea that *consciousness equals meaning.*

The Mysterious Realm of Quantum Mechanics

Einstein called quantum mechanics spooky. And it is true that the weirdness of quantum mechanics demands interpretation. At present, the eight-decades-old Copenhagen interpretation (still the orthodoxy of the discipline of physics) is being increasingly challenged. The many-word interpretation has the world splitting every time you make an observation. Everything possible actually happens, and many "you's" exist in many different worlds.

Another interpretation tells us to just accept that the future determines the past.

Every interpretation today is wild, *and every interpretation encounters consciousness.* Discussing this stuff puts us on the brink of a slippery slope.

Quantum mechanics takes physics beyond the mechanical. *Classical physics* deals with the physical world. *Quantum physics* deals with "observations" of the physical world. Quantum mechanics is the most battle-tested theory in all of science. In eight decades, it has not resulted in a single wrong prediction. But it presents an enigma. It says something mysterious about our world and about our human role within it.

Happily, you need no technical background to face up to the quantum enigma.

When somebody tells you something you can't believe, it's natural to say, "I don't understand." But with the quantum mystery, the big problem is not the understanding. It's the believing.

Quantum mechanics says that before you look, something can be in two places at the same time, and it's your looking that creates it where you happen to find it. And that what someone does in Moscow (or on Mars) can—without any physical force—immediately influence what happens in Toronto or Baghdad.

Strange as this is, we can demonstrate such "magic" in the laboratory. Technological problems limit our display of this strangeness to only small things. But quantum mechanics applies to everything: to baseballs, to the whole universe. The Big Bang was a quantum event. When the physicist who put the biggest thing so far, a large molecule, in two places at the same time was asked, "What's the limit?" he answered, "Only budget."

A Broader World View

Realizing that our planet is not the center of the cosmos goes a long way in shaping our worldview. Accepting that we evolved from lower animals broadens our worldview. Though physics' encounter with consciousness is something we don't understand, it demands a *yet broader* worldview.

Are we Homo sapiens conscious in that we know that we know? Are we *responsible* for our knowing? Having knowledge of *facts* doesn't necessarily mean that you know in the larger, inclusive sense. Knowledge of facts and knowing in the sense of awareness are separate. Knowledge of a kind can be acquired through words and good memory. It does not give you wisdom.

Being *conscious* makes you wise; you are no longer drugged by the world around you. You find yourself awake and aware. You know that you know, and you are full. You find that you have the ability to respond, to be responsible in treating others as you would have them treat you.

Chapter 8

I Need Do No thing

For those who are awake, the cosmos is one.
— Heraclitus, Greek Philosopher, (c. 535-475 BC)

We cannot find God in noise or agitation. Nature: trees, flowers and the grass grow in silence. The stars, the moon and the sun move in silence. What is essential is not what we say but what God tells us and what He tells others through us. In silence He listens to us, in silence He speaks to our souls. Take some time out to be silent with Him."

—Mother Theresa
No Greater Love

If at any time you have had a momentary experience in which you felt compassion, when you felt yourself as part of someone else, then you have experienced being at one with another. Notice that in that moment, you did not feel or see yourself as separate or distant or removed.

This often happens when you first see or hold your newborn child or when you fall in love. You feel that you are melting into another's body, and you just cannot get enough of that closeness. Or you meet someone and recognize him or her as a *soul mate* or as a *twin soul* who seems to mirror all of who you are, and you are instantly comfortable and connected. You meet someone you feel you've known for lifetimes. The connection feels that it exists at a deep soul level. You cannot explain it. You simply feel *at one with.*

It is said that in that moment, whether you are aware of it or not, you are hearing the Voice of God, Life, Cosmic Energy—or call it whatever works for you.

There are no prerequisites for experiencing oneness. You don't even need to believe in a god or higher being. In that moment you have become aware that you are part of something greater. You would give your life for this newborn child, for your family, for this friend or this new love in your life, or for a cause that touches your soul.

In that brief space of time you join the many others who in their hearts have felt that connection, that expansiveness. You have become part of something much larger than self. There is a vision of creativeness, a longing to do something real about making the world a safer place to be, a thirst to quiet the chaos all around us, a hunger for inner peace.

And now, something seems to be happening. Today more than ever, there is a pull, even a sense of urgency to be part of something bigger, something that calls for a movement of humanity in creating the change that will bring us peace. There is a change in the air, and you are part of that change. You are the new air that we breathe.

What Peace Feels Like

In this little book, I am attempting to help you remember what peace feels like, what it is that you already know. Hopefully, it will be a short introduction to a quickened awakening and a readiness to feel and know the quiet center that exists within you. The center—which we call our Higher Power, God, our Inner Christ, our Divine, Life, or however you wish to label *It*—exists. It has always existed but gets easily forgotten in our busy daily-ness because of our life's circumstances. How easily we are lulled into forgetfulness, into this deep sleep that keeps the illusion alive. We are no longer in the driver's seat and in control of our lives or the circumstances in which we find ourselves trapped. The really exciting thing about saying, "Yes! I am ready," or in feeling that connectedness, is that you will discover very quickly *a place within you where you need do nothing, where you rest, where the body ceases to demand attention.* In this place of silence the Voice for God speaks, not in words, not in sounds, but in a deep knowingness, and in this knowingness in which only love exists, you come to know that all the rest that makes your life chaotic is based on fear.

Peace comes when you stop fighting with yourself. Then you can start forgiving you—no one else, this is all about you, you discovering that you are really OK. This peace comes when you recognize that there is absolutely nothing wrong with you; it's just your perception or privileged belief that's making your life difficult. That peace comes when you are no longer at odds with everything, no longer fighting and struggling with the ego—who, by the way, will do everything to retain control. The ego is simply that false self that constantly nags you about not being good enough, seeing to it that you don't escape whatever agenda it is that keeps you in your pain.

So take the blinders off, rein the horses in, get your personality out of the way, see the beauty of your coach, and once more pay attention to your breath. The constant mind talk—the monkeys—will stop, and you will feel this internal quiet, this peace.

How does one shut out this never ending nattering? You begin when you discover that you can't do it all by yourself. When you say to God, (or whatever or whomever) that you need help. It will happen when you decide that you are no longer operating simply on your own agenda, in your own time frame. It will happen one day when you take a moment to be quiet and just sit in your quietness. That will be the moment.

The light—or knowingness—comes on, and you realize that you have kept yourself a prisoner in your own mind, that you have kept yourself from your rightful inheritance of joy and abundance, and that it is up to you to clearly say, "Enough!" That is the moment of lucidity in the dream. It always comes with just one happy realization: *"I need do no thing."*

Rudolf Steiner in his book, *Knowledge of Higher Worlds*, writes about awakening to the Divine within you and strongly suggests that you do nothing, that you don't change anything. Just be in the moment. In that moment are all the answers—whether you listen is up to you. You really need to do nothing except change how you feel about yourself, and then bring others along.

Being, Not Doing, Brings Others Along

I want this truth to stand out like a full moon on a clear night: *an enlightened being is one who shares what she or he knows through who she or he is.*

Not through what he or she thinks or says, but through who that person truly is. A simple little statement: you change *the* world because *your* world *is* changed. You begin to feel differently about yourself, and as you feel differently, you begin to see the world with new eyes. Your circumstances are your circumstances, they don't change unless you change them, but how you see the world and how you see your circumstances totally changes because you no longer have tunnel vision; you are no longer trapped in the prison of your own mind, and as you come out of that prison into the light, your whole world is transformed.

The people in your life also change. We tend to trap people in our minds, to imprison them according to their past behaviour, their history. We anticipate what they will do next, so of course that is what they do; they live up to our expectations, because that is where we have trapped them.

People will treat us according to how we feel about ourselves, and if we feel that we are the victims, that we are wronged, they will treat us accordingly and reinforce our victimese because that is the energy we're giving off. That is the message our body language, our energy, is sending to others. That is who we think we are.

A Story of Change

Allow me to share a story that will give you a better understanding of what I am trying to say. Years ago I was given the gift of a client who, as she shared stories out of her terrible childhood, became a great teacher to me. She grew up on a farm in rural Manitoba, miles from the nearest small town. Her parents would leave each summer to work as cooks at a remote logging camp. They would not return until early winter when snow started to impede the bush roads. The summer she was ten, they left her with $50 to buy food for herself and three younger siblings who were left in her care. The small farm provided chickens, eggs, milk, and a variety of vegetables—that is, if the children tended the garden properly and the good weather held.

The week after her parents left, a notice came in the farm mailbox that the electricity would be cut off if the utility bill were not paid immediately. The bill was $48. She walked to town and was now left with $2 for the remainder of the summer. At ten she was responsible for the care and safety of her young siblings without recourse to any other funds. As she grew older, her parents made more and more demands on her. At fifteen they forced her to marry an older man who was one of her mother's lovers. Soon she was pregnant. After the birth of her second child, she left her abusive husband, took her two children, and fled to the nearest city. She was barely seventeen years old.

She worked, went back to school, and eventually graduated from nursing school. After getting her first marriage annulled, she married a wonderful, loving man who was a great father to her two boys. Her life was good. In her late forties she contacted me. She had been diagnosed with advanced breast cancer. She was approaching her fiftieth birthday, and her husband wanted to host a large party to celebrate her life. He felt that it would be wonderful to have her estranged mother and siblings attend. Her father had passed away years earlier and there had been no reconciliation, no closure, and this had left my client with a gnawing unease.

With her background in oncology and palliative care, she wanted to work on her core issues and longed to walk her spiritual path. She knew that she needed to be at peace within herself in order to assist her body in healing. Over the years she had made attempts to reconcile with her mother and her siblings, but everyone was still too toxic and abusive to be open to any form of healing. Whenever in their presence, she felt physically ill. All the old hurts and abuse would manifest and leave her emotionally drained. She wanted her husband to cancel her birthday celebration, but they both knew this was of major importance in her healing. I suggested that she put into action all the work that we had been doing together over the last several months. Instead of just intellectualizing this *stuff*, it was time to live it—to live in *the now*.

We worked on her seeing her mother in the moment, without the history, without the pain. Knowing that we are all from the same source, I asked her if she were able to see her mother as one of God's angels. "Christ in his many distressing disguises," as Mother Theresa was known to say. We worked and journaled on the importance of forgiving herself and on feeling the presence of others who were guiding and loving her. We looked carefully at what her mother had taught her—mostly what not to do and who not to be—a valuable lesson in being true to herself. Also, having been forced to go it alone those many years, she had learned strong survival techniques. But now, even with the love of a good man, she still felt isolated.

She had to learn to ask for help, and in our work together, she came to know that we are not here alone. She learned that we are surrounded and have always been surrounded with an energy, a loving, guiding energy that is always there. We often need to ask for help, and it will come—sometimes not in the fashion that we would like or choose—nevertheless, it will always be there. It always is. We don't recognize it because of our blinders—our ego and our "privileged" beliefs.

The day of the party, she walked into the room and saw her mother. She saw her with new eyes. She saw her as not separate or apart from herself, but as part of who she was, just in a different body, wearing a different space suit than hers. She saw her as an incredible spiritual teacher of love who had lowered her awareness and who had lost herself in her own darkness, only to awaken in her daughter the thirst of her own spiritual awareness. Her feelings toward this woman were now those of love and compassion.

At that moment, the daughter unlocked the door of her own mind and let her mother out. In so doing, she freed herself from prison as well. Free from her past, she was no longer the victim, and her mother was no longer the persecutor. In that holy instant, everything changed. Because she saw her mother with new eyes, her reaction to her was different; it was now nonjudgemental, and she could only see her with love.

Astonishingly, the mother stood to greet her daughter and did something she had never done in my client's life. She hugged her and told her how very proud she was of her, and how she admired the wonderful life she had created for herself and how fortunate her sons were to have such a wonderful mother.

They were *nice* with each other. And soon, this became a holy relationship because there were no expectations. The next day, the brothers and sisters and their mother all met for lunch and started a journey of wellness as a family. This did not require years of therapy. There were no allegations of child abuse. All the daughter did was to forgive herself at a very deep level of awareness and look upon her mother with new eyes. To date, her cancer is still in remission.

A Book of Tools

My hope for this little book is that through it, I might simply give you some basic tools, some food for thought, little reminders to awaken you to what you already know. I want to assist you in learning how to truly forgive yourself at a deep, loving level of being-ness, and for you to learn to ask for help—help that is always there, reminding you that all you need do is ask.

I also would like to remind you as often as I can that there is and always will be that place of rest to which you can return at any given time, that place that exists within you, not outside of you, not in some far-off Tibetan monastery, but in you. A place deep inside of you where you see and know your perfection, where you have freed yourself from your mind, and where you can just *be*, just show up. Its beauty and serenity will draw you with such intensity that you will be unwilling ever to lose sight of it again.

Its reflection will shine from you, and its truth will draw others into the peace of heaven here. You see, we can choose to stay in the hell of our own making, or we can choose our personal version of heaven, right here, right now. "Heaven" simply is a state of being, and, of course, so is hell. It's right here, right now, and we remain in this hell or purgatory (great holding places in our minds) while we try to sort everything out as we awaken.

John Lennon wrote, "Imagine there's no heaven. It's easy if you try, No hell below us, Above us only sky. Imagine all the people living for today." He was saying that there is no punishment, no hell, and no purgatory. Only what we create for ourselves, what we think we deserve and put ourselves through—hells of our own making.

John was aware that we are creating our own reality, that heaven can be right here, right now, and so can hell. He was aware that this is an illusion of our own creation, that we are trapped in it, stuck in some form of limbo, or purgatory, not quite sure of who we are, where we are, or what we really want. As long as we are trapped there, nothing changes. We are waiting, but not quite sure what we are waiting for.

How difficult is it to let go of our pain, of our suffering? How hard is it to set ourselves free?

It is *damn* hard for most of us!—because our egos keep on running the show. Old tapes keep playing in our heads; they keep us trapped in what happened to us in the past, what was said to us, how badly we were treated. They keep on replaying, saying that we are not good enough, that we don't deserve to be happy, that we have to get even, that we have to be right, to do whatever it takes—even at the cost of our own happiness and safety.

Many of us stay stuck in our prisons because we can't figure out how to free ourselves from our minds. So we mood alter just to cope, just to feel "normal." We usually do this with something or other—an addiction, an obsession, an emotion—that is harmful to our personal well-being. If we understood how simple, how easy it is to be free of all of this, would we let go of our pain, or are we afraid that if we let go, we would no longer have our history and would no longer know who we are?

If I can convince you that this peace, this love, is an easy path, a path on which it's impossible to lose your way, would you choose to stay in your pain, or would you accept your rightful inheritance of love, joy and abundance? It's a simple thing and comes without sacrifice or loss. Once accepted, you are healed, and the power to heal others is also yours. Once you have accepted that you are not separate from your Creator, your god, your own Essence, the gap is gone and you are at peace. "Nothing more than that and nothing less," according to *A Course in Miracles*.

The interesting thing is that it does not cost you anything except a few moments of your time, to be still and to know. "You need do nothing except change how you feel about yourself, and then bring others along."

The Real World

You ask how this works in the "real" world. Well, your "real" world is your illusion, your perception, and you can make it as real as you want it to be. Since you are the only one who can change your perception, then it really is once again how you feel about yourself, and it is up to you to decide when you are ready to leave the prison of your own mind and begin to experience being.

Remember what Parmenides said in 515 B.C.? "... 'Being' is the basic substance and ultimate reality of which all things are composed and motion, change, time, difference, and reality are illusions of the senses."

The world we know is run by people, and you and I are people. The Buddha said, "To him in whom love dwells, the whole world is but one family." When we begin to change how we see ourselves, we see the universe as alive and we are part of this aliveness. We come to understand that we have choice and an ability to shift toward a kinder way of being, a simpler way of living. We have the technology today to communicate this new perceptual paradigm to the mass media and increase the interest in our common future.

How do I, we, us, bring about change? Perhaps now, more than at any time in our history, the choices that we make in our lives have lasting effects and global consequences that will extend for hundreds of generations into our future. In light of the escalating global tensions, recent studies offer new hope and renewed credibility to our most cherished traditions, suggesting that we may be able to "do something" about the seemingly unending cycles of violence and future of our world after all. Recent studies also indicate that there is less violence in the world per capita than ever. Hard to accept but with our electronic media we are made aware of all the violence in the world almost as it is happening.

Research by Gregg Braden [12]and others, as well as the Transcendental Meditation groups, have statistics that show that when a number of people join in a focused, unified consciousness of nondenominational mass prayer, they produce effects that extend well beyond the room or building where the prayer has occurred. So once more, we have information that reinforces that we need "do nothing" outside of ourselves, that the "do something" is within us. As that something within us changes, we change how we see ourselves, and the world heals around us.

In Stephen Post's book *Why Good Things Happen to Good People*, Dr. Post chronicles the link between doing good and living a longer, healthier life. "The science show that we're hardwired to be giving," he says. "We're talking here about a one-a-day vitamin for the soul." A growing number of researchers are supporting his claim with studies that show that the human body benefits from everything from gratitude to generosity. Dr. Post believes that people who want to prolong their lives should work on their attitude, the same way they would change their diet or exercise routines. And he thinks the culture is ready for a shift toward the positive.

Chapter 9

Awakening the Hundredth Monkey

The future enters into us in order to transform itself in us long before it happens.

—Rainer Maria Rilke
German poet, (1875-1926)

This little story has always intrigued me, and I love to share it. It may be true, or it may not. It may be an urban legend, or it may be what change is all about. In any case, even as a parable, it reinforces what I wrote in the last chapter. This little story gives me hope.

It has been told that on a small island north of Japan, a young female monkey dug up a tuber and was rushing off to eat it. (How we know this was a female or what she and the other monkeys did is anybody's guess.) As she leaped to grasp a hanging vine, the tuber fell into a rushing stream directly beneath her. She saw it hung up on a shallow ledge, and she climbed back down to retrieve it. By now, the rushing water had washed the tuber clean. Eating it, she became aware that it tasted much nicer without the soil clinging to it, so she took to regularly washing her tubers in the rushing water.

Soon the other monkeys noticed what she was doing, and being monkeys, they began to mimic her actions. Soon all the monkeys on that small island were washing their tubers before eating them. Then monkeys on the adjoining islands got wind of it somehow and began to do the same. There followed an exponential process that spread until all the monkeys of the world suddenly began to wash their soiled tubers before eating them. And now, I am told, it is a way of life in the monkey world to wash tubers.

Gregg Braden and a few of his colleagues have frequently e-mailed large groups of people asking that we pass on their message for global prayers at a given time. He says, "Statistics have shown that a specific number of people, joined in a focused, unified consciousness of non-denominational mass prayer, produce effects that extend well beyond the room or building where the prayer has occurred."

These studies add to a growing body of evidence suggesting that focusing our feelings and prayers, with the sense that they have already been answered, has a predictable and measurable effect on the quality of life. These findings invite us to feel appreciation and gratitude for peace, as if the peace in our world already exists, and we give thanks for that peace. In this way, we open the door for even greater peace to be present. Scientists suspect that the relationship between mass prayer and the effect of those prayers is due to a phenomenon known as "the field effect of consciousness."

The book, *A Course in Miracles, Manual for Teachers* (Book 3) [13]asks, "Who are God's Teachers?" And it answers, "They come from all religions and from no religion. They are the ones who have answered."

Hearing My Own Call

The call is universal. It goes on all the time everywhere. It calls for teachers to speak for it and redeem the world. Many hear it, "but few will answer. Yet, it is all a matter of time. Everyone will answer in the end, but the end can be a long, long way off"

The idea of a call is not unusual. Many of us have felt a call. The teachings of many faiths speak of a call; to be a minister of a certain denominational church, a pastor, a priest, brother, monk, or nun. In elementary school in the '50s, I remember a prayer card that the nun's gave us when we did well in our catechism class. It was a picture of Jesus carrying a lamb across his shoulders, knocking at a door. The prayer inscription said, "Many are called but few are chosen."

There was a specialness in answering the call. We were led to believe that God had a chosen few—special people who entered the nunnery or priesthood or brotherhood or whatever one's persuasion made available.

As an impressionable young Catholic, like many before me, I was inspired by the stories of the saints. I, too, wanted to give my life to Christ. Since we were not into martyrdom, and since at the age of fifteen I couldn't lead an army and really wasn't too keen on being burned at the stake, I decided to become the bride of Christ. The ultimate love affair that contained all the romance of the stained glass windows, organ music, and the Latin mass called to me. I entered a French Belgian order who had a Mother House in Canada and began studying medicine at a local university. Because the order promoted their work in the Belgian Congo, I dreamed of working in Africa as a medical doctor, and saving all those lost souls.

Since the age of four, I had wanted to be a healer. Medical school and life in a spiritual community was all that I was familiar with, and it naturally seemed the path to follow in my calling to heal.

The call in a nunnery meant to obey and to follow rituals long established in another century. No matter how in love I was with my intended groom, my exuberance and non-stop curiosity, made it difficult for the nuns to tame my personality. To this day, I find it very difficult to take myself too seriously, so you can imagine what I was like then, being so young and energetic and so needing to explore my awakening mind and the world around me. Many times I had to "do" the stations of the cross on my knees or prostrate myself in front of the community and beg their forgiveness for my pranks and buffoonery. Soon the thought of being a nun lost its glamour. As I was leaving God "to go back into the world," the nuns laid a heavy guilt trip on me.

Nun or Householder

Years later, I came to understand that the many boring repetitive rituals in a spiritual community are the same as the boring repetitive rituals of a householder—although, of course, a spiritual community seems more romantic, more special, than that of a householder. Rising at 5 a.m. and going to a cold chapel to recite prayers in Latin over and over again, slowly numbing oneself to the meaning and emotions of the words, doing all the busy daily-ness that has to be done in order to support the religious community, is no different than getting up in the middle of the night with babies, or driving to and from the office doing what you do to put in your day at work, and coming home to load after load of laundry, making meals, washing dishes and floors, driving children here and there, and all that's entailed in running a household and raising a family. I have come to understand that being a householder is a far more challenging and difficult path than being a nun. I have discovered that where you are is really of no great importance—it's all the same.

Throughout the years, I have worked hard at trying to be mellow as a householder and as a working mother. Remaining centered as a spouse and as a mother was a challenge, and attempting to manage a career and stay focused did not come easy. But what I was feeling while doing it transformed it from drudgery and never-ending work into a peaceful meditation. Daily repetitive acts of love are absolutely necessary to maintain one's household and be present for family and business partners.

This point came home to me more clearly one day when sitting a Vipassana, (Buddhist meditation to see things as they really are) and listening to Goenka'ji'. This wise, elderly gentleman from Burma reminded us that being a householder was a most wondrous and difficult spiritual path, and was not to be taken lightly.

So what am I getting at as I ramble on about life in a religious community, life as a householder, a spouse, a parent, and out in the work force? One of my little "epiphanies" was in discovering that it is not in *what* I do that counts, but in how I feel while doing it that makes the difference. I can answer the call there as well as in a cloister. This awareness changed my life at a very deep level, and I began to slowly remove more of the blinders from my eyes.

This is Important Because?

Why do I feel that it is so important to awaken people to their own spiritual awareness? Why is there an underlying urgency? Why is there such a pull today to feel good about ourselves? To be the best we can be? Why is it necessary to search for quality and meaning in our lives? Why do we spend time and energy and money working through and processing our pathology, our understanding of dysfunction, looking inward for answers?

These questions were rarely open for discussion with our parents'/ grandparents' generation, and were classified as family secrets that were to be held close to the chest.

"What are people going to think?" "You have to know your place." "Put it aside and get on with your life." "You made your bed, now you have to lie in it." "You're not going out dressed like that are you?" (I was often guilty of this one with my children) and of course, "We can't get involved—we have to mind our own business!" These thoughts came from another generation, a generation of self-consciousness (with a strangely different meaning than self-*awareness*) that still oftentimes prevails today.

But if we choose not to get involved, we just may lose the life we hold so precious, and our host, Mother Earth, may decide to shrug us off for a time until we evolve further and are ready to try this life again. And yes, we do have to mind our own business—*this* is our business. I think the answer is becoming conscious of our Self in quite another way than our parents were *self-conscious*, and awakening to the truth that what we personally think and do affects all in this global society. Whether we want to be or not, we are part of a large global community, and—pardon the expression—we continue to "shit in our own backyard." The only way I can see our surviving as a healthy, happy species is for each one of us to awaken to herself, and in so doing, become part of the ripple effect that is creating a healthy global consciousness of selves.

So how can we get people interested in being *nice* to themselves and to everyone around them? How can we get more people involved in practising the golden rule? I think I am asking the right questions, so where are all the answers I'm promised.

The Buddha said, "No avoidance, no craving." Which is to say, "Go, experience Life 101, but don't have any expectations." So what was he getting at here, and why should I not expect to have the results I'm working so hard to achieve?

Chapter 10
Prayer and Miracles

There are only two ways to live your life. One is as though nothing is a miracle. The other is as though everything is a miracle.
"—Attributed to Albert Einstein"

... But only one is the way of joy.

There is much talk today about global prayer, and I would like us to examine what our concept of prayer entails. As children, we are taught to pray by kneeling at our bedside, asking God to bless members of the family, memorizing prayers by rote—words and sentences often meaningless and/or misinterpreted by our little minds. We ask God for things we need or want, or we ask him to heal the sick and dying, or to do whatever is pressing at that time. We usually pray because we feel that we need or want something, or feel that we have lack in our lives. In our religious practices, we often pray out loud in an ancient idiom, thinking that God will hear us better if we pray in a language that was around when Jesus of Nazareth was here—or another religious leader.

We have learned to pray quietly, to pray affirmatively, to pray loudly. We learn to pray as an act or intersession for others. We have learned to pray over things, in things, because of things, and in the midst of things. Most of us have been taught to pray *for* things. And indeed, even a prayer of supplication or asking is an affirmative statement that we are open and ready to receive. Some of us, under deep emotional stress and fear, have tried to make bargains with God; that if the Creator will allow so-and-so to live or get us out of this situation, we will enter a monastery or give a large donation to some church or whatever, or that we will stop drugging or drinking or beating or stealing or lying or whatever undesirable thing we find ourselves doing. Many of us have some idea that this Creator, this Divine being many of us call God, exists outside of us and goes about doing our bidding only if we are in his good graces.

It is easier for us to think that we are separate from our god of choice, and not an actual part of this creative force. Many think this energy is separate from us. Or we easily forget that it is within us, not apart or separate. That it is around us and in everything and everybody, without exception. By not remembering, we don't have to take responsibility for our own actions and can rely on some One or some Thing outside of us to save us from ourselves.

It is my conviction that from the beginning of time, the Divine has been a part of creation and has never ever left us even when we felt or thought that we had been totally abandoned because of the atrocities that we've committed or the terrible things that have happened to us. My wise and brilliant editor commented: *OK?* (He had inserted conviction when I had written belief) *There's presently a lot being written and said about Modernism— meaning a time that began with the Enlightenment in which we became certain that this was all a big machine and that with the right instruments, it was only a matter of time until we discovered down to the last detail how the universe works. Now, with Heisenberg's discovery, we know that that's not so, that as British physicist Sir James Jeans suggests, the universe is looking less like a great machine and more like a great thought. Which, I think, is what you're saying. – But with this realization, that the Modern view was wrong, and having moved into what's being called Postmodernism, people distrust unequivocal statements and those who make them. As confident as you may be, you may be ahead not seeming so certain of ultimate reality. So I'm suggesting that you say, "It's my conviction …"[14]*

Prayer Shapes Reality

A Course in Miracles says: "Prayer therefore, brings us into alignment with what already exists within us and opens our minds to the revelation of this existence in the outer world. In other words, what we pray for we already have; but in most cases, we are not aware of it."

William James, an American philosopher and psychologist, one of the founders of pragmatism, and also one of the most influential thinkers of his era (1842-1910), viewed consciousness as actively shaping reality, defined truth as "the expedient" way of thinking, and held that ideas are tools for guiding our future actions rather than being reproductions of our past experiences.

If William James, recognized worldwide as one of the greatest thinkers of his time, validates what I am trying to get across, there may be something very real happening here. We just may have to rethink our thinking. We set up barriers, focusing on all that we don't have, that there is scarcity, that there is not enough for all of us. We repeat our fears over and over again, and so continue to re-create what we feel and are frightened of. We stay locked into events of the past, not in who we are.

There is an old saying, "Don't keep on thinking that way, or what you're thinking will come true." Well, those people who said that were right—even if they *were* our parents. We create our worst fears. We will create and re-create how we feel and what we think. We will continue to draw to us our worst fears. We do not know how to get off this treadmill of our own making.

Prayer—Personal and Up Close

Prayer is a very personal and intimate act. How you pray, when you pray, and why you pray is a direct reflection of your understanding of the Creator and the role that Creator plays in your life. If we are part of God and God is part of us, then that makes us truly Divine. That part of us knows ALL THAT Is, and that part of us called the Divine is in everyone. And I truly mean everyone. So yes, God answers our prayers. Oftentimes not quite in the way we wanted, and we often don't even recognize that our prayers have been answered, but our prayers will always be answered in accordance with the principles of truth and according to our faith or what we personally believe; we will draw to us our truth, and our beliefs will continue to co-create our lives. And yes, this "God" does exist, and this Creative Energy/Allah/Christ/Universe exists in you. Where else would it exist!

Now here is a little catch about prayer. When we stop blaming God and other people for everything that is wrong, and when we become willing to accept responsibility for our lives, our prayers are answered quickly. When you are very specific about what you want, and you do not doubt yourself, and you truly expect a positive outcome, your prayers will be answered. It's simply you being direct with yourself! It's you recognizing that you have to stop trying to control the outcome, and ceasing to worry about it; you are only blocking the natural flow of energy that creates change. Surrender it all—that does not mean giving up. It simply means handing it over and letting the divine power within you answer your prayers without your trying to tell the Divine how to do it.

Fait Accompli

Once you have put it out there and felt the emotions of what you are asking, it has already happened. The Divine does not forget, so you don't have to keep on asking and repeating it over and over again. Accept that it has happened and get on with your life. Each and every time you pray, offer gratitude for All That Is. Begin to live your life in a state of gratitude.

When you see your prayers as having been answered is up to you. *When* you feel worthy at the cellular level that it is your divine right to receive; *when* you are ready to give over control; *when* you surrender fully from your heart—that's when the miracle will happen. Please remember the letting go part. When you hang on to all that *stuff,* when you are filled with your old thoughts and beliefs, there is no room in you for change. Allow, by which I mean create a space to allow change to happen by emptying yourself of old beliefs and past pain and suffering.

The Meaning and Nature of Miracles

A Course in Miracles talks about the meaning of miracles. It says that all miracles are the same. No miracle is bigger or harder to achieve than another. I have often wondered if I can truly get my head around that teaching, but I am definitely giving it my best shot. It means to me that if I can achieve the miracle of finding a parking spot in a major city in front of the building where I need to be, then I can heal myself of any *dis*-ease and bring peace to the world.

A Course in Miracles says, "Miracles occur naturally as expressions of love. The real miracle is that it's love that inspires them. In this sense everything that comes from love is a miracle." The book says that miracles are natural occurrences, and that when they do not happen, something has gone wrong, and that that something has to do with our perception of ourselves.

Prayer is the medium of miracles. It is one way we communicate with the Creator. "Through prayer love is received, and through miracles love is expressed." Our thoughts can and will produce miracles. Where our thoughts are coming from determines the outcome of the miracles. "Miracles undo the past in the present, and thus release the future."

Immanuel Kant, a German philosopher who lived in the seventeen hundreds, possibly the most influential philosopher of modern times, wrote in *The Critique of Pure Reason*, that ideas do not conform to the external world, but rather the world can be known only insofar as it conforms to the "mind's own structure." How you think is what you create or perceive may not be exactly how he intended this statement but it has become the reality of today.

As a younger person, I often found myself in serious discussions, or what my parents called *arguments,* with my younger brother. I would pontificate my "truths," my "beliefs," and he would ask me to prove them. I had no means of proving what "I knew that I knew" This always ended up disastrously because there *was* no proof—no scientific proof and no metaphysical proof. *I just knew*—but trying to describe what I knew produced only words, and of course this created an argument that went nowhere, so for a long time I shared very little that came from deep within me with anyone. I did not know how to do it without the confrontation.

Science and Prayer

The research community has for several years been weighing in on the power-of-prayer debate. Scientists have identified clear links between prayer-like activities and good health. Psychoneuroimmunology, the study of how the central nervous system affects our health, has clearly illustrated the mind-body connection.

Social support, religious activities, and optimism are all associated with maintaining our immune systems. Attitudes that we associate with praying—a sense of hope, connectedness, and purpose—have a measurable positive effect on our natural levels of serotonin, dopamine, and endorphins, all of which make us feel good. And that is exactly what yoga, meditation and antidepressants do for us too.

There's that aspect of prayer in which an individual or group asks a higher power to actually step in and make somebody healthier or to bring peace into their lives. Since the late 1980s, there have been hundreds of studies of intercessory prayer in which people pray for help from a higher being. The grandmother of all these studies is a 1988 project in which Dr. Randolph Byrd, a cardiologist at San Francisco General Hospital, studied 393 patients in the coronary care unit. He placed patients in either a prayed-for group or a control group—a group not being prayed for. The first group was prayed for every day by Christians the patients had never met and who had never met them—and from a distance. After ten months, the patients who were prayed for had fewer symptoms and required less medication than the others. While researchers continue to find links between science and intercessory prayer, believers don't need the lab results. They know by personal experience.

Studies add to a growing body of evidence suggesting that focusing our feelings of appreciation and gratitude, as if our prayers have already been answered, have a measurable effect on the quality of life during the time of the prayer. Clearly there are no right or wrong ways to pray. In its simplest expression, prayer is the very personal and innate ability within each of us to commune with our world, one another, and a greater presence.

Head- and Heart-based Prayer

Prayer obviously is another tool we may embrace to bring change into our lives. If traditional prayer does not interest you, you may want to embrace a form that has no words, no outward expression, and is based simply in feeling. Specifically, this mode of prayer invites us to *feel the appreciation and gratitude* in our heart, as if our prayers have already been answered—even if the world appears to be showing us otherwise.

This is where monitoring the origin of our prayers is important. Evidence suggests that our world and our bodies mirror what we think and feel. Consequently, we must be very clear about seeing to it that our prayers originate from our hearts, rather than in our heads. Here is why: the logic of our brain works in polarity—left brain/right brain, light/dark, good/bad, right/wrong, etc. Praying *for* something creates a strong feeling—a charge— about what "should" or "should not" be. The physics of our world requires that when a thing is created with a charge that has one polarity, the opposite must be created as well, for the sake of balance between the charges.

According to research done by Greg Braden, when we pray "for" something, as in "head-based prayer," we're using a mental process—logic. While these thought-based prayers "for" peace in Iraq, for example, are well-intentioned and appear to create a temporary peace or healing in one place at one point in time, they may inadvertently create precisely the opposite in another place, at another time!

On the other hand, "Heart-based prayer" creates no such opposite reaction. Our hearts have no polarity. In the Native American traditions, there is even a word that describes the non-polar objectiveness of the heart—the heart that sees what *is* rather than judges what *should* be.

The word in Eastern tradition is Shante Ishta, (the single eye of the heart). When we choose peace or healing from our heart, it creates no polarity that has to be balanced; there is no "left" and "right" heart. From our heart, the feeling *is* the prayer! Studies have shown that this quality of gratitude and appreciation for the peace that already exists, creates a "field effect"—in the presence of peace, the only thing that can happen is peace. A point of clarity: this form of prayer is NOT directed at a place, person, organization, country, city, or event. This mode of prayer does NOT attempt to "make" something happen.

The ancients understood that using prayer to impose our will is an abominable misuse of our gift of communion with our world. To impose our idea of what should, or should not be anywhere in the world, or upon another person, is a form of manipulation, and a misuse of this gift. Rather than praying for someone to win or lose, suffer or heal, we have the opportunity to feel appreciation and gratitude for the peace and healing that already exists. The power of this kind of prayer transcends the winner and loser frame of reference. It invites us to elevate the conditions of our world to a new realm beyond win/loss. In accepting this invitation, we open the door to a very subtle, yet powerful principle that allows for the possibility of peace/healing to be present without our imposing our own will to make it so. The principle is simple: in the presence of peace, all that can happen is peace.

Chapter 11
Bringing About Change

Whatever the tasks that your soul has agreed to, whatever its contract with the Universe is, all of the experiences of your life serve to awaken within you the memory of that contract, and to prepare you to fulfill it.

—Gary Zukav

How do I know what my contract with the Universe is? What's the plan, and where do I go or what do I do to find the directions, the road map, to get me there?

Somewhere deep within our psyche, just waiting to be awakened, is the answer. All awareness, all knowledge, all knowingness lies within us. Everything we need to know to allow our soul, our essence, to be free and feel, is ready to be remembered. Tools, memories, knowingness, abundance, everything we need to live in peace and harmony has always been there. The problem is that we have forgotten how to access it. We have bought so deeply into the illusion, into what society teaches us, that we have forgotten what we know from the inside out.

It's time for us to go through a process of unlearning, the process of re-examining what we think we know and how it has contributed to the movie that we find ourselves in.

I am going to take some creative license and repeat what I have often said in my story telling—I've not been able to find where it is written or if it's come to me from an unwritten source—Adam, who according to the Old Testament, upon eating the fruit from the tree of knowledge was thrown out of Paradise by an angry and jealous God, fell into a deep sleep. I have never read that he has ever awakened from this deep sleep. Perhaps we are all actors playing out Adam's worst nightmare, that man is separate and apart from the Creator. This, then, is the original sin—the very thought that we are not a part of the Creator. I feel deeply that if we individually awaken to this truth and pass it on, our movie will change dramatically.

I personally do not believe in an angry or jealous God, but that is *my* truth; it may not be yours, and that's OK. Defining God and attaching human emotions, a form or body and a personality would limit a concept that is beyond defining and make God into a very small, weak being.

What Are We?

As for us? "You are the work of God, and His work is wholly lovable and wholly loving. This is how a man must think of himself in his heart, because this is what he is."

That's me John was writing about. That's you. John, the beloved apostle of Jesus who was inspired by one of the world's great teachers, was writing about us. We are the reflection, the image of the Divine. We are the work of God, and we are lovable and loving. We are incredible heroes to go into such a deep sleep, a great forgetfulness, to leave our source and to forget where we came from. In this act of heroism, we forgot who we are so that we can allow the Creator, Life, Source, God to have a human experience through us.

We have this mind-set, this thinking; "How can I create change? I'm nobody. I have no power." Since all the great masters and teachers have taught that we are made in the image of the Creator, that we are in the mind of God, and that the Divine is within us, we may want to rethink this powerless image of ourselves.

We are this single substance, and that single substance is in everything; therefore we are part of everything. Who or what does that make us? Once more I have to remind myself that this is about me, this is about you. Or do I think that I am so special that this does not include me? Am I so caught in my ego that this can't be about me? That God, the Creator created everyone else equal, in Its image, loving and lovable except me?

Spinoza, (1623-77) a Dutch-born philosopher, presented his view through a mathematical system of deduction, reasoning that all—everything, mind, body, creation—is a single substance, which he called God or nature. In a telegram to a Jewish newspaper in 1929, Einstein wrote, "I believe in Spinoza's God who reveals himself in the harmony of all that exists, but not in a God who concerns himself with the fate and actions of human beings." In Calaprice's The Expanded Quotable Einstein, p. 204 in parentheses in the reference, Calaprice includes these words – "Spinoza reasoned that God and the material world are indistinguishable; the better one understands how the universe works, the closer one comes to God."

We, each and every one of us, have all the power needed to change the world. It is our world. We do not need to travel beyond our backyards. We do not need to read anything, to take any courses, to take any workshops, nor do we need to spend any money unless we feel that it will help us come to know who we are at a deeper cellular level. There are wonderful tools and wonderful awakened teachers who make their living sharing what they know. They have put aside other careers to follow their passion, their soul's path, to assist in awakening others.

A Caveat

Remember though, if you do seek counsel, make sure your counsellors are coming from love, not from fear. If what they say doesn't feel right deep within you—and here I'm not talking about in your ego, but at a very deep and loving level—do not follow them.

Most charge for their services as they too have families to feed and rent to pay. And that's OK. Many of us in that service have been foolish with our money, giving it away irresponsibly. We have "trusted" in God but have foolishly forgotten to "tie our camel." Others have overcharged for their services, creating a problem for those who are truly committed to sharing their gift of healing. We have come to learn that the begging bowl does not work well in our North American economy and life style—nor does wanting too much. Trusting in God or in the universe is a wonderful way of being and is necessary to living a spiritual path, but we often forget that we must take responsibility for our own well-being. And if we have families or partners that we are committed to, we have to be clear that we do no harm in their lives as we pursue our path.

"We need do no thing"—except take time to be quiet enough to know that what we call the Kingdom of Heaven, Nirvana, is right here, right now, and that we are IT.

Passing on the Lie

The rest all exists in our minds. We have all been prisoners in our own minds and created the life that surrounds us, the life based on our own thinking. From our perception of fear, we keep passing on the fear/anger, so that in the illusion, it gets recycled over and over again.

And so we continue to perpetuate the lie we have lived from the time we first dreamed that we were separate from the Creator. Though we have seen glimmers that this is not real, our ego has gotten in the way, and so we create this hell in which we find ourselves. Now it's time to *un*-create it and to live in the paradise that was offered to us in the first place. Then we can have a wonderful experience being human.

A Lucid Dream

When we go to sleep at night, we dream. Every once in a while, we have a *lucid* dream; that is, we know we are dreaming. We can have fun with our lucid dreams, and can create the outcome we want. Perhaps it's time to recognize that this seemingly wakened state of everyday existence is also a dream, and that it too, can be a lucid dream in which we can create the outcome we yearn for.

I shared a conversation with an old friend and asked, "I wonder what would happen if everyone around the world fell asleep, and we all had a change of consciousness. Would we remember what it was like before, or would we forget and create a new now?"

Time, Past and Future, in the Now

If we do live other lives, will we apply what we are learning today in lives yet to come? And if all time is contained in the present moment—as the new physics seems to say—will what we learn today affect the lives that we have *already* lived? Again, if all time is contained in the present, do we *remember* our *future* lives?

But we are stuck in the concept of linear time. We base our history, our story, on that concept, and it is difficult to get our intellect around the idea that all is happening right here, right now—that there really is *only* now! We think in linear time only because we suppose it will keep us from falling off the planet.

Many of us project our futures on certain conditions. We say, "Once everything comes together and so-and-so does this or that or changes, then I will do such and such," or, "If I win the lottery ..." or, "If my mother or father or spouse or child or whomever, does this or that, then I will ..." or, "I can't, because this happened to me," or, "I can't forgive because ..." We are waiting for the right circumstances, the right financial gain, the right people to come into our lives to make everything right, before we give ourselves permission to have the life we so deserve.

According to the new science, all of this is really going on right now, all at the same time. But we are where our consciousness is. We are what we believe. Our life now is a projection of our thoughts, and we have lost the concept of living "in the now." This is New Age thinking; this is real, hard science.

The Dark Illusion

We find ourselves rushing, always trying to "get caught up." We try to sort out our priorities and access what is significant in our lives, and besides that, we are just trying to survive in these times. We are trying to have meaningful relationships with our families or with a lover or spouse or friends, and we can rarely find the time, caught up in a never-ending search for a significant other, a soul mate to fill that loneliness.

Many who are already in a committed relationship feel empty and lonely, waiting for our partner to change or for someone else who will make us feel better about ourselves, desperately hoping to meet someone who will be perfect for us. We are drowning in the never-ending pressures of raising children, and some of us are raising our children's children. Our young people are being greatly influenced by disadvantaged peer groups, by the media, by the escalating violence, anger, and fear that seem to be the norm in their everyday lives.

We seem to be caught racing along on a never-ending treadmill, trying to make headway financially, trying to sort out emotions, often overpowering emotions from our flawed childhood; we have issues with our health, our environment, the water we drink and the very air we breathe. Our bookshelves are heavy with self-help books, spiritual or religious guidance, how to be successful, how to create abundance, etc. We have joined churches, religious groups, cults; we espouse spiritual practices and teachings. Many of us have put up money to attend workshops and seminars and retreats, and have invested our time and energy in those.

We continue searching for something more, something that allows us to feel complete, but it is never enough. We are looking for our path; we are trying to listen to our soul, and the chaos around us is drowning out the Voice for God.

An Awakening

There is a story that the busier Mahatma Gandhi got, the more he meditated, and the more he accomplished. We have all heard the following spiritual sayings "Be still and know that I am God," "Heaven is now," and the words in the New Testament attributed to Jesus "You too can do this and much more."

It has all been said. It has all been written. It is all right here, right now. But we seem to have made the choice of living in the hell of our own making, and most of us feel that some sort of sacrifice has to be made or something given up if we are to truly live our truth. We are desperately trying to find something that we feel we have lost.

Science is beginning to prove that there is something out there that has consciousness that is greater than we can ever comprehend. Through the new physics, we are discovering that there are universes far beyond our imaginings.

That the illusion of time we live in is simply that, an illusion. That all our past, present, and what we call our future is going on right now. That we are where our consciousness is. That we, individually and collectively are creating our reality around us.

If scientists can mathematically equate in numbers what I am trying to say in words maybe, just maybe we are slowly beginning to remember. Something deep inside of us at the core of our being is being stirred. There is a longing within us for better lives, to be the best we can be, to bring peace and joy to this world we live in, and to heal our environment. We want our lives to have meaning. We want to feel that the world is a better place for our having passed through. We are opening up to the concept that we somehow must begin to take responsibility for our thoughts, our feelings, and our actions. As humanity develops its capacity for reflective consciousness, the universe is simultaneously acquiring the ability to look back and reflect upon itself. In coming to understand our spiritual source, we are growing after billions of years of evolution, into a life-form of human evolution that allows the Creator to look at Its creations through the unique perspective and experience of each person. In the word of theologian Thomas Berry, humanity enables the universe to "reflect on and to celebrate itself and its deepest mystery in a special mode of conscious self-awareness.:

Again I quote from *A Course in Miracles, the Manual for Teachers.* "How many people does it take to save the world?" The answer to this question is: one.

> One wholly perfect teacher, whose learning is complete, suffices … It is not really a change; it is a change of mind. Nothing external alters, but everything internal now reflects only the Love of God. God can no longer be feared, for the mind sees no cause for punishment. God's teachers appear to be many, for that is what the world's need is. Yet being joined in one purpose, and one they share with God, how could they be separate from each other? What does it matter if they then appear in many forms? Their minds are one; their joining is complete. And God works through them now as one, for that is what they are.

God's teacher's—that's you my friend, and that is also me. *We* are awakening to *our* truth, *our* knowingness, and sharing our knowledge to nudge and awaken others. Liken it to the proverbial pebble cast into the quiet lake, the ripples moving out farther and farther until they run over the whole surface. As we begin to awaken others, there will be a great many people who will remember their source, who will remember that they too are all from God and that the Creator loves all of his creation equally.

Reaching Critical Mass

If the scientists are right, and if there are enough of us remembering where we came from and who we are—a kind of *critical mass*, as with the one-hundredth monkey—the consciousness of humanity just may change. The world who hosts us just may be healed, restored to her full beauty. Everyone is awakened to what we call the "Christ consciousness"—christus, "another Christ," "one with the Creator," and we begin to remember that we are co-creators, that we are all of the same Creator. Whatever title you are comfortable with, there is only One, and we are IT, we are the mirror image of "god" in human form. And everyone lives happily ever after, blah, blah, blah.

Not quite! Not quite yet!

Why Bother?

How many times have you read this, contemplated and discussed it, prayed over it and meditated on it? Sounds pretty wonderful to me, but again what does it really mean.

What is the "The Law of One"? There is actually a society called The Law of One Society. It is a loosely structured, non-hierarchical network of individuals from around the world dedicated to understanding, exemplifying and practicing the truth we call the Law of One. The Law of One Society is but one incarnation of a long line of groups and spiritual movements past and present that have and continue to spread the universal truth that All is One. They are dedicated to re-awakening this awareness in others by being an example of Oneness and Infinite Love made manifest in their daily lives. Many within their network follow different paths. Some practice different religions or spiritual beliefs. Some find purpose through more practical application of Oneness in our society, while others find it through its more metaphysical aspects. Nevertheless, they are all bound by their awareness and understanding that beyond all belief within the Illusion of Separation there is but one inescapable and underlying Truth – that All is One. It sounds so grand and so impossible. And so unreal.

So what *is* real? If life really is what they quote the Buddha as having said—"Life is hard. Then we die,"—why are we bothering? Why do we strive so hard and get so caught up with trying to grasp a glimmer of happiness, a hope that someone will love us, that people will validate us, that we might belong somewhere? We are raised with the concept that if we work hard, others will recognize us and value us. If we are successful, we will be respected; others will look up to us and be envious. We dream that we may one day win the lottery and never have to worry again. That some saviour is going to rescue us and take care of us if we believe such and such, and the gates of heaven will open to us and we will live happily forever, playing the harp or walking on golden paths, and be forever young.

You know what I think? I think that might get a bit boring after a few thousand years. And what if we're given choices as to what we want to be? To have to decide what age to be stuck in and how we want to look, and whether we want to be male or female, or a cat or a dog or a horse? Rather than that, I enjoy listening to others who think that a mother ship from some galaxy where the beings are benevolent and wise will hover above us and beam us up and remove us from this insanity, and then do whatever's necessary to take care of the rest of the human species.

Others believe that if we chant or eat brown rice or do certain contortions with our bodies and bow and scrape or meditate for hours or repeat rituals or affirmations or the name of God the right number of times, we will become enlightened. True—all of this can keep us entertained until that one day when we're still for a moment and allow ourselves to just be, to just *listen*, to just *hear* the Voice for God.

Some believe they're specially chosen by a jealous and judgmental God, and that all they have to do is obey his ministers or certain religious leaders and interpret the Bible or the Koran or whatever just so, and that even if they feel justified in killing others who don't think the same or look the same or dress the same, if they follow and don't question, they will be saved and part of God's chosen.

Others believe that if they give a large sum of money, they can buy a guaranteed seat in heaven or have all their karma erased. Plenary indulgences of the modern kind. And I have been told by some that God sometimes offers seats on sale (I actually saw this on television and thought it was a comedy routine), and that if we send in 15% of our gross, (it was very clear, our gross—not our net), we get out of the bleachers and closer to God where the angels and our dearly departed sit, and that they will welcome us into His Kingdom. Does any of this make sense to you?

So—what's real and what's wishful thinking? And what bill of goods are we going to buy next? Or better yet, how many wars have been and will be fought over "my god is bigger or better or more powerful than your god"?

Which leads us to this question: over the thousands of years humans have been living on this planet, how many millions have been tortured, murdered, violated, and shunned in the name of an angry god who is different than the murderer's god? How many millions have suffered and starved as the riches of those conquered were taken to build temples or churches to honor the conqueror's god? Treasures and riches that helped create more power and influence, and armed the conqueror's nation in order to defend its own insecure god.

So much of this insanity is still going on, even in our own communities, that it brings us nearly to despair. But no matter how insane, humanity perpetuates the illusion that this is what we must do—just in case.

Time to Wake Up

How do we awaken from Adam's nightmare? How do we change this illusion in which we find ourselves trapped? How do we know what our Essence, our Light, our Soul is trying to remember? How do we know our Selves? How do we know God? How do we differentiate our Ego from the Voice for God—especially since that voice has always been part of us? How do we know what is real and what is not? How do we find out what our plan or path is?

Who am I anyway? Why am I here? And where am I going? And does it really matter? Why is knowing so central to our life journey?

Chapter 12

The Awakening

All you need is love, love. Love is all you need …

—John Lennon

The fruit of faith is love. The fruit of love is service. The fruit of service is peace and serenity.

—Mother Theresa

The Course does not aim at teaching the meaning of love, for that is beyond what can be taught. It does aim, however, at removing the blocks to the awareness of love's presence, which is your natural inheritance. "The opposite of love is fear, but what is all encompassing can have no opposite." Nothing real can be threatened. Nothing unreal exists. Herein lies the peace of God.

—*A Course in Miracles*

I am certain that thousands of beings on the face of this planet are indeed being *nice* to each other. Many are already living the teachings of the master teachers. Jesus the Nazarene taught only love, and so did all the other great teachers.

But love does not sell, at least not the kind of love I'm writing about. It's not sexy. It doesn't make money. But fear does. Fear sells, and it has been the great commodity of power and control that hooks us and keeps us prisoners of our own time and minds.

Our little human minds want to understand, to compartmentalize, to digest as much information as possible, to research, to study, to share knowledge, but we have a hard time allowing for our true knowingness, the knowing that we don't know we have.

Many of us want somebody else to do the work, to tell us what to believe, how to live our lives. We feel that we do not have the time to "be still and know." There are also many of us hoping that a saviour *does* exist, and that he will come and save us and make everything better. Many long for an organization or religion that they can believe in, something that will take care of their needs.

We want our scientists to come up with a pill or technique to make us all healthy and to clean up the planet and maybe create a smart bomb that will wipe out all those who don't think and live as we do.

But it's too easy to focus on those who are not mindful. There are also many people, just like us, some very loving and wise, who are part of congregations and communities that offer love and guidance and support. People who make it a way of life to assist and support others who have less. People who have great generosity of spirit and love for human kind and who quietly go about their daily business being *nice* to all who come into their lives.

There are those who have embraced simplicity and are good stewards of the planet. We do tend to forget that it is people who do all the good things, too—people who are our neighbours, our friends, our colleagues or work mates, our spouses, partners, children, and relatives.

Whatever you do or belong to or join—it's great—as long as it fills you and gives you joy! So live your truth. Have compassion for yourself. Love and honor who you are, and share that with others in whatever manner works for you. As long as what you do is done with joy and integrity, then you have truly found your path, even in this illusion, in this time. I will remind you once more; it is not in what you do that counts; it is how you feel while doing it that makes the difference. And when it no longer feels right, move on.

For many, religion, a spiritual congregation or organization just doesn't at this time seem to be the way or to answer their needs. Past experiences with such groups have proved painful and disappointing.

For others, religious groups of one kind or another seem to be what they need and gives them great comfort and joy. Wonderful! There are many in those groups, though, who would like to put the blame on some supreme being for what happens or doesn't happen to them, and they become dependent on a god who passes judgment and has likes and dislikes for one kind or another of the human species, preferences for some races, preference for the male sex, the color white, a tribe, some countries, some beliefs. We want to be special, to be the chosen ones, to be saved or rescued. The last thing we want is to be responsible for our actions, our feelings, and ourselves. Try to remember once again that this is all just people doing what people do, experiencing humanity, and in doing so, making mistakes.

Our Movie

Think again about this movie we are in; it seems to be made up of many *mis-takes*. It's hard to get even a small segment just right, even a small take, and even then it needs more editing.

It's hard to comprehend the fact that we are creating this movie—creating it with our thoughts and fears. We do not want to accept that our thoughts, our words, our feelings, create our world around us. The Beatles song, "All You Need is Love," says there is nothing new, nothing that you do not know, and nothing that you cannot do when you come from the state of love.

How can they tell me it's easy, that "all you need is love"? What does that really mean? The concept that "love just is" is a hard one to grasp in this that Voltaire called "the best of all possible worlds."

We understand, at least a little, that love is a state of *being*. A state of being. The word *am* is the first person singular of the verb *to be*. Rene Descartes, the French philosopher and scientist, coined the famous, "Cogito, ergo sum"—"I think, therefore I am."

The dictionary says: "Being, the state or quality of having existence; all the qualities constituting one that exists; the essence, or one's basic or essential nature; personality."

Martin Heidegger, (1889-1976), a German philosopher influenced by Kierkegaard, emphasized the need to understand "being," especially the unique ways that humans act in and relate to the world.

Gottama the Wise One, known as the Buddha, wrote that all phenomena are productions of mind and that everything is created by mind. Ordinary beings allow the mind to wander at will, thus enmeshing them in confused and harmful thoughts, but an "examined" mind—an awakening mind, an aware mind—can bring itself under control.

All this to say that to use Descarte's "Cogito ergo sum" collectively, "We think, therefore we are."

The Buddha said that all phenomena originate in the mind, and that when the mind is fully known, all phenomena are fully known.

> For but the mind the world is led; and through the mind karma is piled up, whether good or bad. The mind swings like a firebrand, the mind rears up like a wave, the mind burns like a forest fire, like a great flood, the mind carries all things away. An examined mind thoroughly examines the nature of things, remains in ever-present mindfulness of the activity of the mind, and so does not fall into the mind's power, but the mind comes under control. And with the mind under control, all phenomena are under control …

And interestingly enough, a changed mind changes your world.

What Happens to Us Is Not Who We Are

It is so hard for us to acknowledge that we may be responsible for our lives. That what we see and feel around us may be of our own creation, in our own minds. Remember that our circumstances are ours; they cannot change; what happened to us, happened to us. No one can take that away. But what happened to us is not who we are. As we begin to live in this place that is right here, right now, and as we become more mindful that we are these incredible spiritual beings here to experience being human, we begin to see with different eyes, and we can embrace our humanity.

When we do, everything around us will begin to change. It can't help but change, because *they* are our feelings, *they* are our eyes, and *it* is our perception. How I see and feel about myself will be different. I will no longer be stuck in my victim consciousness. I will no longer be a prisoner of my own mind.

If we all awoke to this, we would send out a different vibration, an energy that changes how people see us or feel about us. Call it whatever you wish—change and you will be giving off wonderful, loving vibes, and the people around you will respond in the same way. They won't be able to help it. You will be radiating love from your center, and this will infect and affect everyone around you. You will begin to see others in a different light because they see you differently.

Mother Theresa said, "I look into your eyes and see Christ in his many distressing disguises."

Ram Das put it *nice*ly when he said, "I look into your eyes and see myself, except a different space suit."

Nirvana, Heaven, that which we are longing for, somewhere *up there*, happens while we experience birth and death right here, right now, within us.

According to the Buddha,

> … Nothing truly exists but the mind, in which there are no images … Therefore they do not know the extent of what has been perceived by the minds of past, present, and future Buddhas, [that's me, that's you, that's us when we become "wise"] and they continue in the conviction that the world extends beyond the range of the mind's purview … and so they keep on rolling … on the wheel of birth and death.

In my work, I often encounter people who are making great sacrifices and enduring personal hardships to pursue a spiritual path. They are leaving for India or Tibet or Jerusalem or wherever, looking for answers. They are living in Ashrams or communities or entering monasteries, hoping to find the answer. Many have discovered the gift of Vipassana (to sit in silence), a retreat, or a journey into the wilderness, all looking for God. All of this is wonderful if it gives you joy and if you do it with clear intent and purpose. But again, many of us are looking for something that is *not* lost, but something that we have perceived as living outside of ourselves. Until we take the time to *"be still and to know"*—without expectations—we will not find the answers. The answers will be and always have been there, right within us, nowhere else. "Be still and know," and get your personality, your ego, out of the way.

My Most Intense Mystical Moment

Albert Einstein wrote: "The fairest thing we can experience is the mysterious. It is the fundamental emotion that stands at the cradle of true art and true science. He who does not know it and can no longer wonder, no longer feel the amazement, is as good as dead, a snuffed-out candle." (Caprice,p.295) most beautiful and profound emotion we can experience is the sensation of the mystical.

These are strong words from such a scientific mind.

My most intense mystical experience, or what I call "my epiphany" happened in a restaurant called Bullwinkle's. According to the dictionary an epiphany is, "a revelatory manifestation of a divine being; a sudden manifestation of the essence or meaning of something; a comprehension or perception of reality by means of a sudden intuitive realization. 'I experienced an epiphany, a spiritual flash that would change the way I viewed myself.' (Frank Maier)."

My experience in the early '80s was at Bullwinkle's, located at that time in redneck country in Alberta, Canada. I don't believe the restaurant still exists, so I cannot go back to my "mountain top" and revisit the place of my awakening. Bullwinkle's was the Canadian version of the American Chunky Cheese family restaurant, with little moveable animals and a continuous water and light show. I was enjoying my favourite pass-time, people-watching, and waiting for the pizza to be ready as my young son played video games nearby.

I guess I zoned out, and the illusion in front of me dissolved. I saw my world for what it is. In that "wrinkle in time," these wonderful human beings appearing in this funny little restaurant had been invited into my life, my movie, and long before I had consciousness. They were present at this time, signed on as extras, as "wallpaper" as it is known in the movie industry, to awaken in me what I already knew. They were all part of my script to help me remember where I came from and who I am. They were all part of me, extensions of myself to trigger a remembrance of my source.

By the time my friend came back with our beer and the pizza, tears were streaming down my face. Explaining what had just happened was not important. I just said, "I know God," and with a very worried look on his face, he nodded and said "that's nice" and poured me a glass of beer.

It wasn't Tibet or India, and I was not sitting at the feet of some great Guru or spiritual teacher. I was not an astronaut returning from space. I was not in some great church or temple or in the middle of the rain forest or out in nature. I had no expectations that great spiritual enlightenment would come to me at Bullwinkle's while I was waiting for a pizza and a mug of beer. But for a brief moment, I found myself totally "in the now," "centered," and it just happened. No fanfare, no lightning bolt, no great master or teacher appearing to me. I was not in any yoga or meditative position, nor had I been fasting or chanting or saying the rosary. It just happened, and in that moment, "I knew." It awakened all that I know, and my flesh and my body dissolved. I was one with ALL THAT IS. I experienced Samadhi, Nirvana, Heaven, and tasted it for a moment. Nothing, no one, can ever take away that experience. It lives within me and fills me. It oozes from my cellular being. It brought back the memory of, "I know what I know."

In Jack Kornfeld's book, *After the Ecstasy, the Laundry*, he says,

> Family is a mirror. In our spouses, our lovers, our parents and children we find our needs and hopes and fears writ large. Intimate relations reach in and touch our history without anaesthesia. The wounds we carry, the longings we have to be nourished are right on the table. They need to be respected.[15]

We can often easily say to family members that we love them, but underneath it all, it is not enough. We also need to be tolerant and respectful of one another. We must learn to extend the same large-hearted spirit to the members of our family that we practice in prayer or in the non-judging awareness of our inner states. We may have to be open to seeing them with new eyes and ask ourselves why we invited certain spouses, certain family members into our movie in the first place. It would be worth asking: "What are they teaching me about myself?" "What am I learning here?" And perhaps it would be wise to ask for help to embrace it and process it so that all may benefit.

Again in Kornfield's book, *After the Ecstasy the Laundry*, a Catholic sister recalls how her years of prayer led her to this:

It has come to one main thing: a willingness to have an ongoing relationship with all good and evil, to allow myself to suffer consciously, to be the tolerant ground that holds the tears of the world, those far and those close around me. My spirituality does not pit itself against anger or passions or conflict anymore. That is garbage. Those teachings have done more harm than good. In the end there comes a realization of no blame. I vow nonviolence to everything. Do not torment, do not escalate pain in myself or outside myself—this has become one of my greatest prayers.[16]

With Tolerance and Without Blame

Tolerance and blamelessness grow when we pay attention to the remarkable and strange qualities in each of the lives we touch. Every person is singular and unique, expressing his or her own nature. Even those who are difficult are living the best they know how.

Heraclitus (c.535-475 BC), the pre-Socratic philosopher quoted earlier, opposed the idea of a single ultimate reality. He believed that all things are in a constant state of change.

And perhaps in a sense they are. We have multiple choices in life—even though many of us think we do not, that we are stuck with only one true path. Yet, each choice takes us down a new path, all towards the same goal. But our choices do determine how easy, how joyful, or how painful and difficult walking our path may be. We can choose this illusion over that illusion.

The Buddha said, "All is change." Change begins with awareness, and awareness begins with me, with you. We are the ones who choose how to react to any given situation. No one can force us to feel or to react. They can push all our buttons, even put us in circumstances where we feel we are out of control, but we are the only ones who can determine how we feel and how we react. We can decide whether a thing is good or bad, right or wrong.

G.E. Moore, (1873-1958), a British philosopher who emphasized what he called the "common sense" views of the reality of material objects, also held that in ethics, goodness is a quality known directly by moral intuition and that it is a fallacy to try to define it in terms of anything else.

Whereas David Hume, (1711-76), a British empiricist, argued against the proofs for God's existence, and in his *A Treatise of Human Nature*, held that moral beliefs have no basis in reason, but are based solely on custom. Both men's arguments are still influential, and both of their perceptions can be correct, for logically, they are not mutually exclusive, but it is your own perception that counts and by which you will live. It is your truth that will set you free. It may not be my truth, and that is OK. It's what works for you.

It's what your consciousness is ready to remember and what you choose to be comfortable with at this time in your own soul's journey.

It is your *understanding of being* that will change your reality—your understanding that influences you to think, speak, and act as you do, and it is your understanding that creates your world. Every moment and every event that you have experienced living on earth has planted something in your soul.

We as a species have yet to be fully evolved but we are learning our way into succeeding stages of spiritual maturity. Experiencing and embracing the full range of living will enable us to touch our truth or The Truth of life, both the pain and the suffering as well as the love and the joy. Everything we do and learn is woven into the living ecology that it the Universe or Creation.

I'll end this chapter by offering a simple tool for decision-making as an evolving human. Ask yourself, "What would an ambassador of God do now?" As you sit with this, again be aware of your breathing, take notice, and ask to see clearly. Ask if there is another way of seeing the situation? Ask yourself, "Am I reacting from fear or from love?" "Am I being mindful or mindless?" Again ask, "Who walks with me?" Say, "Guide and help me with this decision," or, "Show me another way," or, "I could see peace instead of this."

Chapter 13

Living Your Truth

[A lawyer] said to Jesus, "And who is my neighbour?"
Then Jesus answered and said: "A certain man went down from
Jerusalem to Jericho, and fell among thieves, who stripped him of
his clothing, wounded him, and departed, leaving him half dead.
Now by chance a certain priest came down that road. And when he
saw him, he passed by on the other side. Likewise a Levite, when he
arrived at the place, came and looked, and passed by on the other
side. But a certain Samaritan, as he journeyed, came where he was.
And when he saw him, he had compassion. So he went to him and
bandaged his wounds, pouring in oil and wine; and he set him on
his own animal, brought him to an inn, and took care of him. On
the next day, when he departed, he took out two denarii, gave them
to the innkeeper, and said to him, 'Take care of him; and whatever
more you spend, when I come again, I will repay you.' So which of
these three do you think was neighbour to him who fell among the
thieves?"
And he [the lawyer] said, "He who showed mercy on him."
Then Jesus said to him, "Go and do likewise."
—Luke 10: 29-37

Earlier, I mentioned having read somewhere in Rudolf Steiner's book, *Knowledge of Higher Worlds*, something to the effect that once you begin to open to your own truth, it's best not to change anything in your external life.

When I begin to work with people who are opening to their own truth, I ask them for a minimum three-month commitment. I ask them not to leave their relationships unless they are being physically threatened, and not to change anything until they begin to see from a place of love, not fear.

I am always thrilled when they report back how much their lives have changed, how much their partners have changed, or, if their partners have *not* changed, how they are now able to make decisions for themselves from a place of love, not fear.

As you change the way you feel about yourself, your whole world changes. There are no mistakes in the universe, just a lot of free choices—and if you surrender what you cannot control and hand it over to your god of choice, you will allow the Creator to manifest miracles around you. Whether you are willing to accept those miracles or not is another thing. When you begin to live your truth, and when you stop and listen with your heart, your perception changes. It's like a moment of Quaker silence.

The Meaning of Silence

Silence doesn't necessarily mean going into solitude. In the midst of activity, just stop inside. Some of my most profound spiritual awakenings have touched me in the middle of my chaotic surroundings. Just step out of the drama, observe and recognize the movie, the busy-ness, recognize all of it, but don't buy into it. Just observe it. Breathe. Let go. Clear the space. And then come back to the moment and proceed with whatever you are doing or saying, and include that in that space in your heart where you hold only love. It may also help to use the Serenity Prayer that is so integral to the AA movement.

> God, grant me the Serenity to accept the things I cannot change, Courage to change the things I can, and the Wisdom to know the difference.

So what is this all about—the things I can and cannot change? What wisdom do I need to know the difference? We are born, we take on this human form we call our body, and we commit what the Catholic Church calls the original sin which, in my view, is the state of deep sleep—where we have forgotten our source. Most of us have forgotten who we are and where we have come from.

Forgetting

For those of us who have been privileged to witness the miracle of a child's birth and look into the newborn's eyes, we've seen them stare into our souls, and we see love; we see the wisdom of the ancients; we see great curiosity; we see eternity. Then the newborn baby falls asleep and most, upon reawakening have already forgotten who they are and where they came from.

Some, and I am discovering more and more of them lately, hold unto memory. We call these who remember, Indigo or Crystal children. They find themselves trapped in this form, this vehicle, this space suit that does not work very well, equipped with a very primitive communication system, and are desperate to reach their "soul group."

Whether we choose our circumstances—such as time and place, parents, gender, family, genetics, or even whether the body functions properly—we are still here, participants in this dream. Some of us catch glimmers of the dream and begin to manipulate the dream to our advantage, but most of us go on in a deep sleep, prisoners enslaved by our own minds. We go through life living out the assumptions imposed on us by those who came before us.

Our Agreement—Why We're Here

Don Michel Ruiz puts this quite clearly in his little book, *The Four Agreements*. In the beginning, he talks about "The Prelude to a New Dream."

> You need a very strong will in order to adopt the Four Agreements— but if you can begin to live your life with these agreements, the transformation in your life will be amazing. You will see the drama of hell disappear right before your very eyes. Instead of living in a dream of hell, you will be creating a new dream—your personal dream of heaven.[17]

The new science is creating more proof that all time—ALL time—exists in this moment. All is happening that has happened or will happen and it *is now*, right here, this moment. Where we are, who we are, why we are, and where we are going is *now*. If this is all just a dream, what are we to do? If it's a memory of what already is—for many, a nightmare—that we feel we cannot escape from, can we really do anything about it?

What if each of us is a perfect spiritual being who in a great act of love has taken on human form to allow the Creator to have a human experience through us? What if we are all ambassadors representing the Creator here on Earth? What if we all have the tools, "the right stuff," to be everything we can be? What if we have knowingness of everything, far beyond the comprehension of our limited brainpower, and what if we put that knowingness to use and unlock ALL THAT Is for a nanosecond? Fragments of memory will come back; where we came from, who we are, and why and what we are doing here. And then we can go home, back to our source, which we now know that we never left; we just got trapped in an illusion or time warp or in a dream, and got stuck, waiting for someone to nudge and probe us a bit to wake us up, and as we awaken we create nirvana—our heaven on Earth.

So if we are ALL THAT Is, what are we doing here in the first place? And if we are co-creators, why is this place so chaotic and painful, and why is there so much injustice and disparity amongst ambassadors for God? I think the answer is *free choice*. The ability to freely choose is responsible for this mess we're in.

So how can we become more aware that what we think, what we think we see, what we do, has consequences? That it makes up the life around us? And, if we have *free choice*, why did we take on our particular role in this movie in the first place?

Can you imagine what the essence or soul of the being that came as Hitler would have said before taking on form? *"I choose to do what? ... So humankind can begin to recognize man's inhumanity to man on a global scale?"* Hitler was made in the image of the Creator. Hitler is/was a spiritual being having a human experience.

Can you begin to comprehend what an act of great love towards his fellow travelers he must have felt to go into this incredible darkness and take on the human form and personality, Adolph Hitler, and to live out those circumstances, and to truly forget that he too is an angel of God? That "his path" was to teach us about forgiveness at such a deep level that it affected our world, our relationships, our possessions, our children, and our consciousness? And what about the millions of victims who gave their lives under terrible inhuman conditions as an act of love for the good of the whole. If we are one, we are all part of Hitler and his actions, and we are all part of Jesus the Nazarene, and of the Buddha (the wise one) and of all those that gave their lives to assist us in our awakening. We are all terrorists, victims, saints, sinners, and angels alike.

Looking at the Script

If we are the creator of this dream, this movie we find ourselves in, and if it all exists in our minds, maybe it's time we take a good look at the script and the plot and the outcome and do a major rewrite. Most of us have not been too successful at raising the funds to financially back the movie we would like to act in. Maybe it is time we became a little more aware of our words, our actions and reactions, our thinking, and, most of all, of our feelings.

What has happened to us is what has happened to us. Whether we choose to sit in Calcutta with a begging bowl, be in the never-ending rat race of our present economic life style, or choose to contemplate our navel in some cave in the Himalayas, we are still in this soup together. But what happened to us—what our life's circumstances are—is not who *we are*. But most of us stay buried in our pathology and are fearful of letting go because we have based our persona on past events. We are captive—even though with deep pain—in the prison of our own mind, and if I should let that go, I ask, without my history, who would I be?

An Extraordinary Figure

Allow me to share another story with you. Nearly twenty-five hundred years ago, a young man sat under a tree in northern India, determined to find a way to transcend the sufferings that he recognized as endemic to the world. Born a prince named Siddhartha Gautama in a small kingdom in what is today southern Nepal, he had renounced his royal heritage in order to escape the cycle of birth, death, and rebirth that inevitably leads to suffering, loss, and pain. As he sat under the tree, he recognized that all of the world's problems begin with a fundamental ignorance (*avidya*) that causes beings to misunderstand the true nature of reality. Because of this, they engage in actions that lead to their own suffering and fail to recognize what leads to happiness.

Siddhartha remained in meditation throughout the night, and during this time, the veils of ignorance lifted from his perception. He came to understand how the lives of all beings in the world are constantly influenced by their own actions (*karma*), and that seeking happiness within the changing phenomena of the mundane world is a fundamental mistake. He saw everything in the world as impermanent (*anitya*) and understood that because of constant change, even things that seem to provide happiness—such as wealth, fame, power, sex, relationships—are in fact sources of suffering (*duhkha*). In addition, he perceived that everything comes into being dependent upon causes and conditions—a doctrine referred to in Buddhism as "dependent arising" (*pratitya-samutpada*)—and he understood that because phenomena are in a constant state of flux, there is no enduring essence underlying them. Nor is there a supreme being who oversees the process of change and decides the fates of beings. Rather, every being is responsible for its own destiny, and the entire system of universal interdependent causation is driven by its own internal forces. Individual beings are what they are because of the actions they performed in the past.

Chapter 14

Dreaming a New Dream

My Law

—Unknown

The sun may be clouded, yet ever the sun
Will sweep on its course till the cycle is run,
And when into chaos the system is hurled,
Again shall the Builder reshape a new world.
Your path may be clouded, uncertain your goal:
Move on, for your orbit is fixed to your soul.
And though it may lead into darkness of night,
The torch of the Builder shall give it new light.
You were. You will be! And know this while you are,
Your spirit has travelled both long and afar.
It came from the Source; to the Source it returns.
The Spark which was lighted eternally burns.
It slept in a jewel. It leapt in a wave.
It roamed in the forest. It rose from the grave.
It took on strange garbs for long eons of years,
And now in the soul of yourself, It appears.
From body to body your spirit speeds on.
It seeks a new form when the old one has gone.
The form that it finds is the fabric you wrought
On the loom of the mind from the fibre of Thought.
As dew is drawn upwards, in rain to descend,
Your thoughts drift away and in Destiny blend.
You cannot escape them, for petty or great,
Or evil or noble, they fashion your Fate.
Somewhere on some planet, sometime and somehow,
Your life will reflect all those thoughts of your Now.
My Law is unerring; no blood can atone.
The structure you build, you will live in—alone.

107

From cycle to cycle, through time and through space,
Your lives with your longing will ever keep pace,
And that that you ask for, and all you desire
Must come at your bidding, as flame out of fire.
Once list to that Voice and all tumult is done-
Your life is the Life of the Infinite One.
In the hurrying race, you are conscious of pause
With love for the purpose, and love for the Cause.
You are your own Devil, you are your own God.
You fashioned the paths that your footsteps have trod.
And no one can save you from Error or Sin
Until you have hark'd to the Spirit within.

The Voice

To create our new dream, to change our lives and do what we have come to do, to know our path; this will come about when we completely forgive all we have done to harm ourselves. And we will forgive ourselves only when we take time to hear the quiet Voice from within—and recognize that it speaks from love.

The Voice speaks to everyone who wants to listen, most times not in words, but in feelings of knowingness. It speaks all that we are willing to hear. Often, though, we do not *want* to hear; perhaps afraid that it will tell us to give up something, or afraid that we are so sinful, it will not talk to us at all or perhaps we are afraid that It wants something from us. But ALL THAT IS is not an immature child who shuts us out or makes any demands. Sin has nothing to do with whether the Voice will speak to us or not; remember that sin is simply the lack of love toward out selves – it has nothing to do with God. The Voice is always there; our hearing has to do with putting our egos aside and hearing.

It's a matter, too, of learning the art of listening, of recognizing the Voice in what we hear everyday. It's always speaking; it's not going anywhere—anywhere except where you are, and it will wait until you are ready. It can afford to wait; it has eternity on ITS side. The Voice does not tell you what to do or not to do. It does not dictate your life and how you should live it. It does not control or command you. It does not judge you or reward you.

The Voice speaks only *from* love and *of* love. It guides you only *in* love. It fills you only *with* love. It protects and nourishes you with love. It speaks in a gentle, loving silence—perhaps when you are deeply distraught. When you have put your life in danger, it may speak with loud urgency. But however it speaks, it will grab your attention when you are ready to listen.

We are open to hearing the Voice through others who are helpers-along-the-way, voices speaking only in love and with guidance, never dictating, but sharing what they know from their own perspectives, not better or more knowledgeable than other human beings, just different, with wisdom worthy of being listened to and embracing.

But here is another caveat; always question the source and then choose, remembering who you are. In mistaking another's voice for *the* Voice, we make that other responsible for our feelings and for our perception of who we are. Each time we allow a loved one or a stranger or acquaintance to say or do something that hurts us deeply, we set up a pattern that locks us in. Don't let another prevent you from forgiving yourself. Forgiving yourself is the starting point. *Deep* forgiveness—the kind that will free you from all the hurt and pain of self-abandonment.

By putting the inner Voice above the external voices, we free all others in our lives and beyond. No one can hurt us anymore. We no longer give our power, our feelings, our sense of self away to another. We reclaim our self—our Self.

As hard as this concept is to believe, if this world is a world that we have co-created, then it's all about me, all about you, all about us. As we change our self-perception and learn self-forgiveness, we will be open to hearing the Voice for God. And listening, new as the sound of the Voice may be to us, if in response, we, with vigorous honesty, look at our illusions, we will reclaim our true selves.

Putting Yourself First

What is the difference between being selfish and being self*less*? Or better put, *creatively selfish*? Yes, better put, because the Self never goes away; it is us. Being selfish you put your feelings and wants and needs ahead of everyone else from a perception of fear and self survival. You are under the delusion that someone wants something from you and that there is not enough so you hoard your feelings, your emotions, your possessions 'just in case' and make it about 'me first.' Being self*less* you know Self and your actions come from love. You see your 'self' in everyone and everything around you and you act and react in the state of love.

Letting Go

Many of us—perhaps most of us—are not prepared to let go. We don't want to let go of who we think we are. Or of our pain, our loneliness, or of our feelings of abandonment. It is all we think we know. Someone—I don't recall who—said, "I ain't much, baby, but I'm all I got." Crudely put, but it's the way we mistakenly feel.

We may insist on repeating our painful experiences over and over again before we're finally willing to let go and say, "No more! I will no longer try to tell my god how to run the universe. The juggling has become too complicated. I'm just too tired. It's time to surrender!"

But when you do surrender, you'll find there is something very liberating about it! About *"letting go and letting God."*

That does not mean that you give up and lie around waiting for your god to do something for you. No white knights will come riding into your living room to rescue you. You just surrender. You hand it all back. "Here, God—or Cosmic Betty or Buddha—take it away. I have had enough! I give it back to the source." Then you begin to ask for help and guidance in everything you do and refuse to draw the negative things to you any longer. You begin the process of *for*-giving and giving to yourself, *moi*. With this, you begin a new dream.

We Can't Do It Alone

Healthy people recognize that we cannot do this alone. It's something we do together. Forgiving ourselves may mean finding a therapist or a pastor or someone who knows and practices the art of listening. *We* honor our sadness, *we* talk about what happened to *us*, about *our* feelings, *our* circumstances, *our* choices, *our* fears and *we* will process them and free *ourselves* of *our* past.

To dream this new dream, some may even find it necessary to explore other lifetimes. Deep in our cellular structure, our Karma guides us; Karma simply being life itself presenting the experiences that give the soul opportunities to grow. These karmic experiences repeat themselves over and over again, one repetition often being more painful than the one before, until we make every relationship a holy relationship, every feeling, every action and reaction and interaction, one of love. That is called forgiving ourselves, "for giving to our self."

In Jack Kornfeld's book, *After the Ecstasy, the Laundry*, he says,

> Karma, the cause and results of every action, comes from the heart's intentions that precede each action. When our intentions are kind, the karmic result is very different from when they are greedy and aggressive. If we are not aware, we will unconsciously act out of habit and fear. But if we attend to our intentions, we can notice if they spring from the body of fear or from our deliberate thoughtfulness and care.[18]

Once we begin to process our past and see it for what it is, only our past, we may give ourselves permission to free ourselves from it. We will then awaken to our Self, step beyond our individual ego, and connect with the Divine within us, our Higher Power, our Inner Christ, our Truth. Once we make that connection, we will be naturally drawn back to our fellow human travelers along the way, to those who are sharing this planet with us, those who are written into our movie. We will feel the sustenance from the universe, and because we are awakening, we will see the potential for an awakening in each person we meet.

We will come to know our Dharma, a Buddhist term referring to the natural law or cosmic order of all things, including the moral principles that apply to all beings and things. How do we live our Dharma? How do we apply right conduct to where we are and what we do? Our Dharma represents the eternal truth and the teachings that can bring liberation.

Where do you go to rediscover who you are? Where do you go for guidance and quiet in order to recognize your path?

There are many paths—religion, spirituality, nature, service, contemplative life, work, family, community, creative art, and the like. Each of these paths could bring you to your truth. And all that your truth is is love. It may come in this or that guise, but it will all lead to love of your self. Everything else is based on fear.

A Community of Awakened Minds

As we become more aware of who we are, we will seek out those of like mind. It may happen consciously or through a wonderful synchronicity that just presents itself. Maybe I should say that synchronicity has to do with two or more events coming together at the same time, fortuitously, yet not linked by any apparent cause. You may want to read what C. G. Jung, the great Swiss psychiatrist who founded the analytical school of psychology had to say about it.

Synchronistically—without apparent cause—we will find compatible people being drawn to us in the most unusual places and ways. Perhaps only in a momentary greeting, or it may be for a short period of time, and perhaps for a lasting relationship. We attract what we know. We draw to us those of like mind, and when the encounter comes, there will be an ease, a soul recognition. We will touch each other's lives, sometimes with just a smile, the brush of a hand, a word of greeting, but when it happens, we know. We will feel compelled to recognize the Divinity in another and we will draw the human family together in common enterprise. We are being beckoned to continue unfolding our capacity for reflective consciousness, both individually and culturally, so that we might learn how to live consciously and compassionately with our fellow travellers. That is the challenge and the promise of our journey.

Our Creativity

Creativity is the invisible source behind all things seen. It is the ability of human beings to bring forth onto the physical/visible level that which is conceived in the mental/invisible level (consciously or unconsciously) and the emotional level.

These words I've just written showed up on my computer one day. I am not sure if they came from me or someone else, and if not from me, I apologize to whoever wrote them. Much of what I write just happens. Often I am not sure if *I* wrote what I wrote, or if it comes from something I have read somewhere—but I am just letting it happen as I sit in front of this little screen. So if this belongs to someone else, my apologies.

But back to creativity. God infused us with the power to conceive, express, and enjoy the fruits of our creative power. We create through thought, word, and deed. Although few instructions accompany this ability, it is conceivable that we are each here to reveal the creative ideal of the Divine. This not only translates into artistic creativity, it also has to do with our ability to create a world environment that reflects divine ideals such as love, peace, abundance, joy, harmony, and power. I think that that last one power is where we get a bit confused. Instead of using our power to create divinely, we create by default things we don t want, because we do not understand how to use our divine creative power.

Life unfolds from the inside to the outside. The how and why really doesn't matter, and would be beyond my ability to explain. But I'm not making this up; many have explored the theory of creation for centuries and have determined that it really does work.

A very enlightened teacher one who does not embody a space suit such as ours spoke to me one day, and said,

> Your predictions and expectations are self-fulfilling. Since your consciousness (thoughts) creates your universe, all you have to do to change your world is to change your consciousness!

Unfortunately, our thoughts have created a nightmare—perhaps, as we said, Adam's nightmare. We find ourselves living in it, and most of us do not know how to awaken from this terror. In fact, we believe that the pattern of this dreadful world cannot be broken or changed.

What We Have Created

Perhaps we should take a serious look at what we have done—at what we sometimes do.

To adversely affect the world around you, or to affect another person, you don't even have to speak you negative thoughts out loud. If you think it hard enough, the person toward whom your thoughts are directed may hate you or be afraid of you, and yet not be able to explain why. In some cases, people actually *feel* what you think about them. That is how powerful we are. That is how powerful our thoughts are.

Thought + Words + Action = Results. That is the creation process. Every second of our lives, we are creating individually and collectively. Because we are not taught how powerful our creative potential is, we go ahead and think wrongly, and experience the results of what we think but would not have dared say. These thoughts in turn evoke a fearful or unloving response from others. Soon, our thoughts unfold as words. Words inspire action. Action creates the environmental conditions we all experience.

We can all find explanations and excuses outside of ourselves in order to rationally explain many of the challenges we face in life. Yet, as we grow spiritually and as our understanding evolves and we awaken, we cannot evade the fact that we are made in the image and likeness of God. The point here is that God is creative, therefore, I am creative. The simple fact that I breathe links my mind to the mind of God! Simply because I think! Simply because I am and I know that I am!

Mind produces ideas that crystallize as thoughts. Our energy ripples out like a stone dropped in a pond and the ripples impact other people. This is true about me, and it is true about you. It is also true that we have created a pretty ugly world.

Our Hope

But there is hope. And that hope lies in a simple correction process that puts our innate creativity to a much better use. Start each day by seeing the day the way you want it to be. See yourself handling every responsibility peacefully and effectively. Trust that when the results you desire do not show up immediately, they will eventually show up. Start again. Remember that you can start your day any time you want; it is your day.

See yourself with a smile on your face and joy in your heart. You can rely on the fact that others will be affected by your peace and joy. In those moments when you are caught off guard and are angry or frightened, breathe deeply; focus on your breathing and say to yourself, I can see peace instead of this. Correct your thoughts and feelings, and be clear that they come from love.

Remember, you are a very creative force. Do not feed the situation with destructive thoughts and feelings; you will only add to the negativity, and you will reinforce fear that will only escalate. Be mindful, be conscious of the light that surrounds and feeds you with love in every breath you take. The Divine Love is within you, and you are divine; remember this. Use your powerful creativity to bring peace to this situation and to honor the Divine in youself as well as in those around you. Do this in your quiet place deep within you; do this in your silence. It will not always be easy, but remember, the more damaging and destructive the ways in which a person behaves, the greater is their cry for healing and correction. As you learn to create sacred quiet space within yourself, you will allow change to happen. If you are full of fear, there is no space for love.

The universe uses you as its device of creativity, and through you, the Divine can transform any situation into a corrective healing experience. Be willing to be used as a creative instrument of divine healing and evolution. If what I just said is not clear, please re-read it; it will change your life and the lives of all who come in contact with you.

How do we change this world into a place of peace instead of fear? How do we change the consciousness of humankind so that we can bring heaven right here, right now instead of this hell or our own making? *Your success in changing the world depends on one thing; your willingness to practice taking little steps every day.* Each day you will take more and more steps, until they become a way of life. And as your willingness increases, and you take these steps with joy and with your heart wide-open, you will stop dreaming your nightmares of judgment and begin to dream dreams of forgiveness that will take you out of your pain and fear.

As you slowly incorporate these steps of forgiveness into each moment, they will become a habit, and when you are under stress or facing fear or confrontation, they will be a part of you—tools ready for whatever need arises.

Remember This Morning?

This morning when you awoke, you took a moment to offer gratitude for yourself—just your being here today changed your world. To be is to show up, and you, in a heroic act of love, have shown up. So be grateful simply for your being here, and for being aware that you are waking into this wondrous illusion at this most interesting time.

As you went about your day, you learned that having begun it by going into that special place inside of you—being still and knowing that God is God—your day was different. Whenever you forgot, you started your day again. Your object was to remember, and in the remembering, you began to form a habit. You thought about the kind of day you wanted, and told yourself there was a way in which this very day could happen just like that.

Now continue to do the same in the days to come. If you consciously start your days in gratitude the moment you awaken, you will set the tone for the entire day. Try everyday to have the day you want. If you find that you are strongly resisting that state of gratitude, and your ego keeps on getting in the way and reinforcing the idea that you can't be grateful, then you are not ready. *Do not fight yourself.* Just start again, and when you feel yourself getting stronger, say, "Today I will make no decisions by myself." This means that you are choosing not to be the judge of what to do. But it must also mean you will not judge the situations in which you will be called upon to make a response. Throughout the day, any time you think of it, have a quiet moment for reflection; tell yourself that you can attain the kind of day you want; the feelings you would have, the things you want to happen to you, and the things you want to experience, and say, "If I make no decisions by myself, this is the day that will be given me."

If your circumstances allow, spend time in meditation. Remember that it is not so much in the rituals you perform or in the length of time you take to do them; it is in the feeling of quiet in that moment when you connect with God. If you have the luxury of forty-five minutes in the morning and the same at night, what a wonderful gift you have given yourself. But if your life's circumstances are such that you have only a few moments of personal quiet in which you can just *be*, that is wonderful also.

Just try to remember during the day to connect quietly to the Creator within you. This can be done at any time, anywhere, under any circumstances. No special rituals necessary, no special candles, no special mantra, no special diet or body stance—just you and your Creator at any time and any place, under any circumstances. That means in the shower or bath, in the john as you sit or stand, while you dress or feed your family, and while you make your way to work or school or whatever you are headed on this day.

If you find yourself being caught up in fear and doubt, refresh yourself and remember once again the day you want, and recognize that something has interfered. Do this as soon as you realize that you doubt yourself and that your fear is getting in the way. If you do not like the way you are feeling, and if you are holding onto your doubts, you can remind yourself what kind of day you would like and start over again.

The Need to Be Right

As you begin to realize that your happiness does not depend on your being right, you will find that you are at a turning point in your awakening. So many of us live by the saying "I would rather be right than happy!" that we miss out on the joy of life. It's time to give that up. *This tiny grain of wisdom—all by itself—will allow you to honestly look at the world and everyone in it differently.* Now at least you have an open mind and you are willing to be shown. "Perhaps there is another way to look at this," you say. "What can I lose by asking?"

It is easier to have a happy day if you prevent unhappiness from entering at all, but we are just beginning to see through the illusion and we are just beginning to acknowledge that just maybe we are not alone.

At the beginning of your day, you said, "Today I will make no decisions by myself." You gave yourself a gift—the freedom to internally ask advice before you decided on anything. You and your internal adviser would agree on what you wanted before it could occur.

"It is but this agreement that permits all things to happen. Nothing can be caused without some form of union, be it with a dream of judgment or the Voice for God."

Decisions bring results because they are not made in isolation. You and your adviser make them, for yourself and for the world as well. "The day you want, you offer to the world, for it will be what you have asked for, and will reinforce your adviser's rule in the world. Whose kingdom is the world for you today? What kind of day will you decide to have?" That reflects back to the very beginning of the book when you asked: "Where will you have me go? What will you have me do? What will you have me say and to whom?"

Sharing Your Moment

The one we call Jesus the Christ—Jesus who is one with God—is reported to have said: "When there is more than one gathered in my name, I too shall be there."

So share that moment with another; you too are the Christ—the one with God. Share that moment with someone you can trust who will not mock or make little of *your* truth, *your* belief.

> It needs but two who would have happiness this day to promise it to all the world. It needs but two to understand that they cannot decide alone, to guarantee the joy they asked for it will be wholly shared. For they have understood the basic law that makes decision powerful, and gives it all the effects that it will ever have. It needs but two. These two

are joined before there can be a decision. Let this be the one thing that you keep in mind, and you will have the day you want, and give it to the world by having it yourself. Your judgment has been lifted from the world by your decision for a happy day. And as you have received, so must you give.[19]

So who do you ask to join you in having a happy day? Who is that one you can trust? Do you feel you're being asked to go out and evangelize as though you were a "born again Christian," or a member of a church or cult, and work the crowd on the street, asking people to join you in sharing your personal truth? No, that's neither necessary nor suggested. There is only One that you need, and that is the Voice for God; the one spoken of as the Holy Spirit, the Creator or the Life Force. Remember that these names and titles are simply symbols for a force or life far greater than our little minds can comprehend. So you see, you need not do anything. You need not preach anything; you need not "soldier gather," or have others stand with you while you pray or prophesy loudly all that you think you know.

> Do you not understand that to oppose the Holy Spirit is to fight yourself? Think about this. He tells you but your will; He speaks for you. In His Divinity is but your own. And all He knows is but your knowledge, saved for you that you may do your will through Him. God asks you do your will. He joins with you. He did not set His Kingdom up alone. And heaven itself but represents your will, where everything created is for you. No spark of life but was created with your glad consent, as you would have it be. And not one thought that God has ever had but waited for your blessings to be born. God is no enemy to you. He asks no more than that He hear you call Him "Friend."[20]

What an incredible, moving gift being offered to us! God Is simply because of you. The Creator set this all in motion because of you. There is an agreement pattern between you and the life force we call God—this agreement pattern was totally by your own consent—you have only forgotten and gotten way off track. God is here to do *your* will—not ITs will—yours! What a concept. How wonderful to do *your* will! You are the most important being in this wonderful universe created just for you. Now that is freedom. There is nothing else that ever should be called by freedom's name. Unless you do your will, you are not free. And would God/Source/Universe … leave ITs creation—you—without what he has chosen for himself?

> Now hear God speak to you, through Him Who is His Voice and yours as well, reminding you that it is not your will to hate and be a prisoner to fear, a slave to death, a little creature with a little life. Your will is boundless; it is not your will that it be bound. What lies in you

has joined with God Himself in all creation's birth. Remember Him who has created you, and through your will, created everything. Not one created thing but gives you thanks, for it is by your will that it was born. No light of heaven shines except for you, for it was set in heaven by your will. For it is by your will the world is given freedom. God turns to you to ask the world be saved, for by our own salvation, it is healed.[21]

I am asking you to give yourself a gift: the gift of a life of peace, the gift of a life of abundance, the gift of a life of wellness, and the gift of a life of joy. It is your natural inheritance. All the rest, we have created in our own minds through fear, based on *our* perception from *our* personality, *our* ego, *our* life's circumstances and *our* domestication.

How are you to give yourself this gift with all of our preconceived ideas, our assumptions, our responsibilities, and the chaos and injustice around us? How do we become *creatively selfish* without causing any more damage in our lives and to those lives around us, especially in our families and to those we are intimate with?

Mother Theresa in her book, *No Greater Love*, says,

We cannot find God in noise or agitation. Nature: trees, flowers and grass grow in silence. The stars, the moon and the sun move in silence. What is essential is not what we say but what God tells us and what He tells others through us. In silence He listens to us; in silence He speaks to our souls. Take some time out to be silent with Him.

Start by staying quiet enough to ask for help. As often as you can during the busy day, try to connect to that which is constant within you, that part we call your center, your sanctuary, where only love is. Remind yourself as often as you need, that you are an ambassador for God, and ask what a loving god—one with a very a human personality—would do in this given situation. Practice what the prophets taught about treating everyone as you would have them treat you. That goes a long way towards changing one's actions and reactions. You are a spiritual being here to have a human experience. If you screw up, make amends in whatever way you can, in whatever way works for you that does not cause more damage, and get on with life's next experience. Don't stand in your own way.

Remember. You need change nothing except your perception about yourself. Once you forgive yourself at a deep cellular level, your world changes. Once you remember and embrace who you are and why you are here, everything changes. Everyone around you changes. The world is changed. You have brought peace to the world, and everyone in your world is saved. You have created a new dream, your dream.

Chapter 15

Finally Home for Dinner

If there is light in the soul,
There will be beauty in the person.
If there is beauty in the person,
There will be harmony in the home.
If there is harmony in the home,
There will be order in the nation.
If there is order in the nation,
There will be peace in the world.

Unknown

Your working day is over. Whether you have a spouse, partner, family, friends to go home to, or are living alone, take a moment before you enter your place of dwelling—or the local pub for a drink, or the gym, or your second job—and just take a moment to reflect before you end that part of your day.

For a brief moment, wherever you are, try to be still. Allow me to help you relax. Be still and become aware of your breathing. Become aware of you. Check your body. Are you tense? Are you uptight? Are you angry? Are you in pain? Are you emotionally drained or hurting? Take that breath, that *prahna*, that life force, and feel it coming into your body. Make a conscious effort to feel it penetrating every cell of your being, relaxing you, calming you, healing you. You can visualize it as a color, a feeling, a sound—whatever works for you. If you're tense, squeeze every muscle in your body as you breathe in, and as you breathe out, relax—let it all go. If you really need to hang on to your pain, to your tiredness, to your depression, then relish it; enjoy your negativity, your *dis*-ease. It's yours; you own it and no one can take it away from you except you … it's yours to hang onto or yours to let go. You have free choice; you are in charge.

You may feel that your life is the pits at the moment, a lot of bad things may have happened during the course of the day, or you are holding on to *stuff* that happened yesterday, last month, last year, whenever—it's still just *stuff*, but it's not happening this very moment; it's in the past. Now it's up to you whether you want to hang on to it or let it go. Just try to remember if you can that it's not happening right now. Yes, it may have happened only an hour ago or yesterday, but right here, right now, all I am asking is that you pay attention to your breathing and enjoy it for the moment. Dedicate a moment of silence just to honoring yourself—no one else. You deserve this breather, for you have just survived another day of heroism in human form.

Now if you are ready to truly forgive yourself and begin to have the life you are entitled to, feel the presence of the Divine within you, hear the Voice for God in your heart. Feel Love's presence, hear the Voice—remembering that you may not hear it every moment, maybe not tomorrow, but you will hear it. Just start forgiving yourself one moment at a time.

There is no doubt that it will happen. It took you a while to learn a new instrument, a new language, perhaps to master a computer program. It took time to gain or lose those extra pounds, or to build up all that muscle, or to do what you do so well—whatever it is. So give this a chance; it's like anything else, once you practice and do it regularly it becomes second nature, and all of a sudden you experience ALL THAT IS.

With this knowledge, do you really think you will go back to who you were not? Or to your pain and fear, to that hole in your soul that beckons you into the darkness of despair? Back to those soul-destroying feelings of abandonment? How much longer do you want to drown in a Dismal Swamp of your own making? Or are you willing to give yourself a chance to start again, to recreate your life, to rewrite your script, and eventually find yourself in a new movie—one more to your liking—and to come home to your Self?

So Begin

Begin by processing your past and seeing it for what it is, remembering that it is *just* your past. Once you free yourself from it, you will awaken to your Self, step beyond your individual ego, and begin to connect with that part that I call the Divine within you—your Higher Power, your Inner Christ.

Once you make that connection, you will be naturally drawn back to your fellow human travelers and see them with new eyes. You will begin to interact in a new way with those who are presently sharing this planet with you, and you will remember that they are all part of you.

You will look on those who are written into your script and acting in your movie, and you will feel sustenance from the universe, and this will nourish you. It will fill you, and you will be able to choose how you interact and how you see—you will choose for perhaps for the first time in your life.

Because you are awakening, you will see the potential for the awakening of each and every being in the world—from the drug addict on the street to the politician on the front page of your paper, to the terrorists that hold you prisoner in your own time. You will choose once again. You will come to know your Dharma, in Buddhism, the natural law or cosmic order of the universe, including the moral principles that apply to all beings and things. Your Dharma represents the eternal truth and the teachings that can bring liberation.

So How Do You Live Your Dharma?

How do you apply right conduct to your present circumstances and to what you now do?

First find a place inside of you that holds only peace, only love, and hold on to it, trying to reconnect as much as you can during the busy-ness of your day. Remember the affirmation from *A Course in Miracles*? "Nothing real can be threatened. Nothing unreal exists. Herein lies the Peace of God."

As you become more aware, you will seek out those of like mind. You will find your tribe—your soul group, and you will begin to work as a community of awakened beings, even though you may never meet in the physical. You will connect with their energy. You will know that they are there supporting you as you are supporting them. There will be a connection, a joining of hearts of people of like mind, a profound sense of homecoming. That does not mean that we will come to live together in communities or groups, or leave our spouses and marry someone else of like mind—for some of us, that might be our path—but there will be a connection, a joining of hearts who are coming to live their truth

As you live your life according to the teachings of the great masters, your life will change; it can't *help* but change. You will touch the lives of others, and their lives will change, and that never-ending ripple will continue throughout the universe and far into universes beyond our comprehension and imagination, and the little world we live in will change. Simply because you have chosen to live in the state of love rather than fear. You are living according to what your soul longs to do. You are comfortable and accepting of who you are. You are assisting in bringing us into a wonderful age of enlightenment simply because you are honoring yourself.

Spiritual traditions throughout history have affirmed that we are created from life-energy whose essential nature is love. It is our core essence, at the very heart and center of our experience. Because love is at the center of all, we are able to make friends with ourselves and others. Teilhard de Chardin wrote that the only way for billions of diverse individuals to love one another is "by knowing themselves all to be centered upon a single 'super-center' common to all." The love that is the life-energy of the Universe provides that common center for us all.

A New Day

There is a readiness. In Buddhist mythology, it is said that each new era is served by a Buddha who offers a perfect form of teaching for that time. *Maitreya*, the Buddha of Love, is the name given to the Buddha who will next appear on Earth.

However, Zen Master Thich Nhat Hanh has said that this next Buddha may not appear in the form of a single awakened individual. As our understanding of interdependence grows, he says, "The next Buddha may be the Sangha itself." That means that we will collectively be helping one another awaken. *We* are the Buddha. *We* are the Christus. *We* are the Promised One.

In Duane Elgin's book Promise Ahead (A Vision of Hope and Action for Humanity's Future) he writes: "*We are fulfilling the purpose for which the cosmos was created. We are the agents of evolution, enabling the Mother Universe to reflect upon, and then to surpass herself creatively. We are not becoming angels and saints; we will simply be awake to the fullness of who and what we already are. Just as reaching adulthood marks the beginning of creative work in the world for individuals, attaining our early adulthood as a planetary civilisation will mark the beginning of a new phase in humanity's exploration and learning.*"[22]

I have often said to my students that the second coming of Christ, the one talked about in Christian teachings, is perhaps us awakening to being our own Christus that we also are 'the anointed one'. As we awaken, we come to know that we are One with God. Even the one we call Jesus taught very clearly "*That they all may be one; as thou, Father, art in me, and I in thee, that they also may be one in us: that the world may believe that thou hast sent me and the glory which thou gavest me I have given them; that they may be one, even as we are one: I in them, and thou in me, that they may be made perfect in one; and that the world may know that thou has sent me, and hast loved them, as thou hast loved me*". John17:21,22 &23.

The greater the number participating in this that we do, the greater the acceleration of the effect. (Remember the story of the hundredth monkey?) It takes only a very few people to make a difference in an entire world. Perhaps this is the "mustard seed" of the parable that Jesus used to demonstrate the amount of faith required of his followers. Have we forgotten that with a very small number of committed people, the world can and will change? "The harvest is abundant, but the workers are few." With such potential, what are the implications of such a collective power advancing on the great challenges of our time?

Elgin wrote in 2000: *"We are entering a time of great opportunity – and of great peril. Although the test of our evolutionary intelligence has already begun, I believe it will be another decade or two before a momentous initiation and great turning will manifest with full force and produce consequences that will reverberate into the deep future. Future generations will look back on the actions we take in these years before the initiation and will reflect on how we rise to meet the challenge of living through one of the most stressful pivotal, exciting and important times in human history".*

But remember, start with small steps. That's all we can do. Each step takes us closer to living mindfully. Remember that there are no mistakes, simply experiences along the way. You are now home for dinner—figuratively and literally. You will be nourished and full—both in earthly terms and in spiritual terms. This all starts with you. No one can step into your shoes and have your experience and do it for you. Which is to say, you *are* the "light of the world." The light is in your soul. In knowing this, notice the impact on your household. Remain mindful. Bring harmony into your home, and this will carry out into your community. The new physics describes light as the basic building block of material reality. David Bohm has described matter as "condensed or frozen light" and that light is the fundamental building block of our cosmos. It is interesting that, according to the Gospel of Thomas, when Jesus was asked by a disciple to describe where he came from, he replied: "We came from the light, the place where the light came into being on its own accord and established itself." Elsewhere in this same gospel, Jesus says: "Whoever has ears, let him ear. There is light within a man of light, and it lights up the whole world." In Eastern traditions, we find similar descriptions that we are beings of light. In Buddhism, the awakened consciousness is described with phrases such as "self-luminous recognition."

The Moment of Truth

You have had had a long day, you may be tired or you may be exhilarated. You may have a spouse, children, family or friends who want a piece of you the moment you walk in the door. You may live alone and appreciate your refuge and silence, or you may need to fill it with sound and distractions.

How can you stay centered and give to others when you are feeling depleted, under stress, and there are so many who want a piece of you? What can you do to reclaim yourself?

Once more go back to your breathing. Find your center. Feel the love in your heart; after all, it's yours; now send that love out to those who demand your time—despite the chaos happening all around you. Be still as you observe your movie. Be still and listen to what each person is projecting either by words or body language. Each and every one around you is needing, longing to be acknowledged, to be validated, to know that someone sees them, and that they have been heard and recognized. If you feel you can't handle this situation without an unpleasant reaction, go back to your breathing. "Perhaps I can see this in another way," you say to yourself, and once again try to see these people with your new eyes. After all, that these people surround you is no coincidence. Long before you appeared on this earthly scene, you invited them into your movie to teach you about yourself.

If your spouse, or child, or even your dog is irritating you, and you want to respond or react in anger ask, "What am I learning about myself in this moment of the now?" Ask for guidance and ask yourself, "How would a mindful being see this? What would a co-creator do with these circumstances in order to bring peace and harmony to this situation? How can this scenario heal me of old memories, old tapes of fear and pain?"

This is pretty hard stuff—to stand there trying to reclaim your center and not react in anger and in fear. This is pretty heroic stuff, too, but remember, you made a decision to save the world—and since it is *your* world, you are the only one who can change it. You are the hero in your own movie.

Be truthful with yourself. If you are depleted and have nothing left to give, say "I am empty at the moment, and I have no way of resolving this, but I will listen, and hopefully, I will hear what you are asking of me." Use whatever tools you have for a non-violent communication. Use and project the love and peace that exists within you. Ask for all the help you can get. Ask your Creator to assist you in acting and reacting in the best way to bring peace to this situation.

Remember, no one can make you react. People can push your buttons and attack your vulnerability and your tiredness, but you own the feelings, the actions, and the reactions. And yet, what can you, who are just now remembering that you are a co-creator, do to create harmony? It's like the secret of doing well in real estate. Instead of "location, location, location," bringing light and harmony into your home is "attitude, attitude, attitude." Or rename it perception or mindfulness.

Once more at the end of your day, take a moment for gratitude—towards yourself and everyone you're interacting with. If you have the time, create a gratitude journal and write down three things you are grateful for right here, right now. Every evening, add more to your gratitude list. They don't have to be major—just little things that gave you pleasure during the day.

If you find that you have the gift of quiet and time, sit with yourself and focus on your breathing once again. Have a "conversation with your god of choice," and talk about your day. Expose yourself totally, the strengths you've noticed about yourself as well as your weaknesses. Talk about your fears as well as your dreams. Share your disappointments as well as your successes. Explore your sorrow as well as your joy. Acknowledge how difficult it is to be a good ambassador for God, a good co-creator, and once again ask for all the help you can get in being all that you can be. Just remember to get your personality, your ego, out of the way and expose all of yourself. Be free and vulnerable and childlike.

Remember that this god of your choice is your friend, your confidant, and your mentor. There is no judgement here, you're just sharing yourself with someone or something that loves you unconditionally and knows everything. If you are tense or stressed out, do the same breathing exercises you did in the morning.

My friend who does not wear a space suit such as ours said to me one day:

> Tell your people and tell them now—you can only do what you have come to do when you are in complete forgiveness of all you have done to hurt and harm yourself. Yes, we do mean each time you let a loved one say and do something that hurts you deeply. Each of you has allowed this as a pattern in your life. You see why forgiving yourselves is the starting point. This is deep forgiveness we ask for. The kind that when you go there you feel all the hurt and pain of your abandonment of yourself. It is the kind of awareness that stops the negative forces in your lives. We ask the most difficult thing imaginable. We ask that you put yourselves first. And by this action you free all others in your lives and beyond.

Because our conscious recognizes that we are here now and have chosen to awaken to our 'Self' being alive at this time confers on us all a unique responsibility as well as a unique opportunity. At the beginning of this book I did a "Buyer Beware". I mentioned that as you awakened you cannot go back. As Duane Elgin writes in Promise Ahead: "We are now "on duty" and responsible for preserving the evolutionary integrity of the human experiment. We are the leaders we have been waiting for. We are the social innovators and entrepreneurs we have been seeking. We are the ones who are challenged to self-organize and pull ourselves up by our own bootstraps…There is Promise Ahead."

Sit or lie down or just get comfortable, and allow each breath to bring in that freedom and love that is your inherent right and fill your heart with it. Begin to let it fill your body so that every part of you remembers that you are loved and very loving. Allow your breath to seep outside of your body, surrounding you as if you are being cocooned and wrapped in an energy of love. This is yours to own.

Now, begin to fill the room and extend it throughout your house or building. This love will embrace all who are there. Now project it out to all who live in your community, your town or city, and your country. Fill all the countries of the world and all of those who live in this world, no matter what species or form, color or belief, enemy or friend, with your love.

Embrace all of humanity, and I do mean all; embrace every living thing on this planet with love. Now expand it outward until Mother Earth is in your belly, and you are in the Milky Way. With each breath you take, your love will expand and fill your universe and all the universes far beyond your imagining.

Imagine that: with each breath you take, it fills you with the love of who you are and that love touches All That Is, and ALL THAT IS is within you.

Feel it. That is who you are. That is who and what you *truly* are. Slowly bring this love back into your being and have it settle in, filling your heart.

Just before you fall asleep, once more offer gratitude to yourself as you have chosen to embody human form, to co-create, to allow the Creator to have a human experience through you. This is big; this is huge; this is love.

As you end your day of an awakening life, bless yourself, and from your heart, from the depth of your being, say with love and truth, "May all beings be happy; may all beings be free."

You, my friend, have just changed the world. And because of you and all who embrace the love of who they are, the world is saved.

Blessings to all of you, and thank you for co-creating my movie.

Namaste!

References & Bibliography

Chapter One: Whose World is this Anyway?

1. Newberg, Andrew B. M.D and Waldman, Mark Robert. *Why we Believe What We Believe.* Free Press. A Division of Simon & Shuster, 2007

Chapter Four: Changing Our Perceptions through Changing Our Minds

2. Robbins, Tom. *Fierce Invalids Home From Hot Climates.* Bantam Press, 2001

3. Bakan, Joel. *The Corporation: The Pathological Pursuit of Profit and Power.* Viking Canada 2001 Paperback Penguin 2004

4. Elgin, Duane. *Voluntary Simplicity: Toward a Way of Life that is Outwardly Simple, Inwardly Rich.* Revived Edition . Quill, William Morrow. An Imprint of HarperCollins Publishers. New York. 1993

5. Elgin, Duane. *Voluntary Simplicity: Toward a Way of Life that is Outwardly Simple, Inwardly Rich.* Revived Edition . Quill, William Morrow, An Imprint of HarperCollins Publishers. New York. 1993

Chapter Five: Creating Change in our Business and Corporations

6. Korten, David. *When Corporations Rule the World.* Kumorian Press, Inc. and Berrett – Koehler Publishers, Inc. 2001

7. Maich, Steve. *The Internet Sucks.* Maclain's Magazine, Canada. October 2006

8. Harmon, Willis. *Global Mind Change: The Promise of the 21st Century.* Revised and expanded 2nd Edition. Berrett-Koehler Publishers & Institute of Noetic Science. 1998

Chapter Seven: Understanding Consciousness and Responsibility: The Ability to Respond

9.   Twyman, James. *Portrait of the Master.* Findhorn Press. Independent Publishing Group 2000.

10. Elgin, Duane. *Promises Ahead: A Vision of Hope and Action for Humanity's Future.* Quill. An Imprint of HarperCollins Publishers 2000

11. Monbiot, George. *Heat: How to Stop the Planet from Burning.* South End Press. 2007

12. Braden, Gregg. *The Isaiah Effect: Decoding the Lost Science of Prayer and Prophecy.* Three Rivers Press. Member of the Crown Publishing Group. Random House, Inc. 2000

Chapter Nine: Awakening the Hundredth Monkey

13. *A Course in Miracles. Foundation for Inner Peace.* Book 1. A Course In Miracles Text. Book 2. A Course In Miracles Workbook for Students. Book 3. A Course In Miracles Manual for Teachers. Public Domain. Published by the Penguin Group.

Chapter Ten: Prayer and Miracles

14. Durham, Charles. Freelance Editor

Chapter Twelve: The Awakening

15. Kornfeld, Jack. *After the Ecstasy, the Laundry: How the Heart Grows Wise on the Spiritual Path.* Bantam Books. 2000

16. Kornfeld, Jack. *After the Ec*stasy, the Laundry: How the Hear*t Grows Wise on the Spiritual Path.* Bantam Books. 2000

Chapter Thirteen: Living Your Truth

17. Ruiz, Don Miguel. *The Four Agreements: A Practical Guide to Personal Freedom.* Amber-Allen Publishing. 2001

Chapter Fourteen: Dreaming a New Dream

18. Kornfeld, Jack. *After the Ecstasy, the Laundry: How the Heart Grows Wise on the Spiritual Path.* Bantam Books. 2000

19. *A Course in Miracles. Foundation for Inner Peace.* Book 1. A Course In Miracles Text. Book 2. A Course In Miracles Workbook for Students. Book 3. A Course In Miracles Manual for Teachers. Public Domain. Published by the Penguin Group.

20. *A Course in Miracles. Foundation for Inner Peace.* Book 1. A Course In Miracles Text. Book 2. A Course In Miracles Workbook for Students. Book 3. A Course In Miracles Manual for Teachers. Public Domain. Published by the Penguin Group.

21. *A Course in Miracles. Foundation for Inner Peace.* Book 1. A Course In Miracles Text. Book 2. A Course In Miracles Workbook for Students. Book 3. A Course In Miracles Manual for Teachers. Public Domain. Published by the Penguin Group.

Chapter Fifteen: Finally Home for Dinner

22. Elgin, Duane. *Promises Ahead: A Vision of Hope and Action for Humanity's Future.* Quill. An Imprint of HarperCollins Publishers 2000